STEP BY STEP TO BUYING AND SELLING YOUR HOME

DAVID ORANGE
BSc (Est Man) FRICS

foulsham
LONDON • NEW YORK • TORONTO • SYDNEY

foulsham
The Publishing House, Bennetts Close,
Cippenham, Slough, Berkshire, SL1 5AP, England

While every effort has been made to ensure
the accuracy of all the information contained
within this book, neither the author nor the
publisher can be liable for any errors.
In particular, since laws change from time to
time, it is vital that each individual should
check relevant legal details for themselves.
No responsibility or loss occasioned to any
person acting or refraining from action as a
result of any material included in this
publication can be accepted by the author or
publisher. The views expressed and conclusions
drawn are the personal views of the author.
Examples used in the text are illustrative only.

Forms on pages 132–52 reproduced in
the original book *Make Money Selling Your Home*
by kind permission of The Law Society.

ISBN 0-572-02690-0

Typeset by ABM Typographics Ltd, Hull.
Printed in Great Britain by St. Edmundsbury Press,
Bury St. Edmunds, Suffolk.

ABOUT THE AUTHOR

David Orange BSc (Est Man) FRICS, is well qualified to write this book.

David became a partner in a top Midlands firm of estate agents at the age of 25. Within five years he was the managing director and owner of the eight-office company. At the peak of the eighties property boom he sold out to one of the country's largest insurance companies. He went on to be one of the highest-paid estate agents in the country.

In this book David offers totally impartial advice based on his wide experience, with the aim of saving every reader buying or selling their home hundreds of pounds.

ACKNOWLEDGEMENTS

I would like to thank the following people for
their assistance and advice in writing this book:

Steven Morewood, BA (Hons) Humanities, PhD
David Smith
D. Nicholas Bowen

DEDICATION

This book is dedicated to my parents John and
Esther Orange

CONTENTS

INTRODUCTION

Buying or selling your home will be one of the biggest steps you will ever take. Despite the property slump of the early 1990s, most Britons still aspire to buying their own home and to moving upmarket, given the right financial circumstances.

Part one of this book deals with *buying your home*. We discuss what you should buy; the legal points; mortagage; financial matters; the valuation and survey.

Part two is about *selling your home*. In this part you will find answers to questions regarding the general considerations when selling; maintenance and presentation; methods of sale; dealing with offers; and negotiating.

This book will provide you with the right advice and guide you through the buying and selling procedures, step-by-step, stage-by-stage. With it, you can benefit from my experience, be aware of the pitfalls, and in that way, avoid falling into them. You stand to save yourself a considerable amount of both trouble and money.

PART 1

BUYING YOUR HOME

CHAPTER 1

HOW, WHERE AND WHAT TO BUY

HOW, WHERE AND WHAT TO BUY

Key money-saving points

1 You can save a large sum of money by negotiating hard. Ask probing questions of sellers and their estate agent to help you in your negotiations. If you are a first-time buyer, then you are in a particularly strong position.

2 You can save a lot of money by buying when the property market is slow, particularly during winter months.

3 You can save a small fortune by buying a dirty, empty or neglected property. It may cost you thousands of pounds less than similar properties in reasonable order. A modest sum spent on improvements can take the value back up considerably, netting you a large profit should you decide to sell.[1]

4 If you have a house to sell, sell it first so you are in a strong negotiating position on your new purchase. The saving you make could amount to thousands of pounds

The steps to follow when buying a house

Step 1 Consider what type of mortgage you will have and how much you can borrow; read Chapter 3 carefully.

Step 2 Visit estate agents, study newspapers and look at areas and houses that may interest you; see page 13.

Step 3 Talk to your solicitor and get an idea of legal fees; see Chapter 2.

Step 4 If you have a house to sell place it on the market. Until you have a prospective buyer interested, you will probably not be able to go much further towards buying; read

[1] However, a word of warning here – do make sure you know how much needs spending on the property to bring it back up to scratch, before you go ahead and buy.

Part 2 – Selling Your Home.

Step 5 Study the buying and condition checklists before making an offer on the home of your choice; see page 16.

Step 6 Finalise your mortgage application and consider the type(s) of survey you will have; read Chapters 3 and 4.

Step 7 Notify solicitors; The legal procedure takes place as described in Chapter 2.

Step 8 If the survey and legalities proceed satisfactorily exchange contracts; see Chapter 4.

Step 9 Legally complete your purchase and move in!

How to buy your chosen home

Once you have made the decision to buy, my advice would be to start looking at once. Having considered the area (see page 21), the first thing to do is to drive around your favoured location in search of 'for sale' notices. At the same time, not every property on the market will display a 'for sale' board, so to make sure that you cover the whole field of available houses you should also check out the property papers and local newspapers.

It is also essential that you visit and keep visiting local estate agents. Although many of them profess to offer a mailing list, in practice few operate one very successfully. This failing is quite understandable – mailing lists are costly to operate and rarely sell houses! We are all individuals with different tastes in property. While, therefore, it is a good idea to register your interest with particular estate agents, don't make the mistake of sitting back from

that point on. Sure, some obliging agents will agree to telephone you with details of houses that come on to the market, but not all of them will do so and even the most dedicated and patient are unlikely to keep ringing if you continue to spurn their advances. Further, if you wait for the mailshot to arrive, then especially when houses are selling well, you risk losing out to other buyers who are prepared to be much more active.

This may come as a surprise, but in my experience many prospective buyers have no more than a vague idea of what they are looking for and more importantly, they don't know what they are likely to get. It is recommended that you actually go along and view certain properties. Use my checklist as a guide (see page 16). That way, you will become more knowledgeable about just what you are looking for and what makes a good buy.

Dealing with estate agents when buying your home

It is very important to remember that an estate agent is duty bound to look after his client's best interests. This means the seller. Obviously, he will want to get on well with you and hopefully persuade you to buy a property from him, but do not fall into the trap of confiding too much to the agent, no matter how friendly he might seem.

When prospective buyers used to come to my office or ring up to make an offer over the 'phone, my response would be to enquire whether they were prepared to increase their bid if the client refused it. In a good many instances they would agree on the spot, such was their desire to secure the particular property. But they had given away their ace card, before the game had even begun! The reaction of any estate agent would be to pass on this information to his client, in effect, giving the vendor much more negotiating strength. In the process the purchaser may end up having to pay more.

The special position of a first-time buyer

It you are a first-time buyer you can be in a very strong negotiating position. In the section on financial services we will see how a first-time buyer can obtain special money saving advantages when taking out a mortgage.

Let's briefly consider the strong cards a first-time buyer can play. Most sales hinge on a first-time buyer. If a chain of sales is long it will need a first-time, or cash buyer at the bottom. So it is possible for a first-time buyer to negotiate a price reduction because they can proceed quickly and clearly. A further option may be open to them. The top seller in a chain may not be able to reduce the price by much. However, if, say, four houses hinged on the deal, the other parties or each party in the chain might be prepared to put some money in a 'pot'. Say the offer was £2000 less than the asking price, each seller, by reducing by £500 each, could get the sale away and the whole chain moving. An astute solicitor or estate agent involved in the chain could perhaps identify this situation with some investigation. It is better, though, to mention this to your solicitor or the estate agent at the bottom of the chain.

Sell your own home first

While first-time buyers have an advantage, those with a house to sell are not in a strong position to buy another house until their own is sold. Once you have decided to move, you should therefore put your own property on the market.

In rare circumstances, your own home might be suitable for the vendor and a direct swap can be negotiated. Should the vendor be uncertain you might offer to show them your home and try to convince them that it has the right ingredients to sell quickly. Alternatively, you can part-exchange your existing house through buying your new home from a builder, though generally you need to be moving upmarket.

> Don't fall in love. Too many people are guilty of believing a viewed property is already theirs before they have seen a contract let alone signed one! Too often grave disappointment, even depression, is the outcome when the sale falls through. Above all, you must be realistic and philosophical about the house-buying business. Never move in mentally until contracts are exchanged. Beware, too, that because of this premature emotional attachment, rash and ill-advised judgements are often made. Save money by not going out buying items for your 'new' home until it is actually yours.

The buying checklist

When you are likely to view several different houses in a day it is important to make a note of what you actually saw so that you can make accurate comparisons. Hence my checklist which I suggest you use for each property you consider seriously.

For houses that you feel you are very interested in, fill in the further checklist on the condition of the house if you wish.

Although there is much truth in the saying 'one instinctively knows when something is right', the golden rule is, *never* decide to buy a house on a first visit. If you do, you could come to regret your decision. Don't let your emotions take over. First impressions are important, to be sure, but you may well have missed some important points which the checklist will bring out. Therefore, review the property at least once more with the aid of the checklist.

Try and judge the house as a house, ignoring the obvious inducements put on by the seller. Discount the presence of, say, expensive furniture and consider how your belongings would look in their place.

THE BUYING CHECKLIST: THINGS TO CONSIDER

1 Address of house?	**7** Council Tax Assessment £ Band?
2 Location? (a) Schools (b) Shops (c) Pubs (d) Recreational facilities (e) Public Transport	**8** Copy of bills? (a) Heating (b) Lighting (electricity) (c) Gas
3 Any serious location drawbacks? (a) Pubs too near (b) Under main flight path (c) Electricity pylons too close (d) Poor or dated design (e) Next to factory or commercial building (f) Other	**9** All services connected? (a) Burglar alarm (b) Central heating
	10 Fixtures and fittings to be left? (a) Kitchen appliances (b) Light fittings (c) Curtains and carpets
4 Future Appreciation? (a) Stability of neighbourhood (b) Individuality of houses (c) Will the house sell readily in the future	**11** Where does the sun rise and set?
	12 Size of rear garden and is it south facing?
5 Internal and external condition?	**13** Freehold or leasehold?
	14 Price?
6 Accommodation? (see property particulars sheet)	**15** Agent's name and address?
	16 Agent's and property telephone numbers?

Useful questions to ask the seller and his estate agent

1 How long has the house been on the market?

This could provide vital clues as to whether the price is likely to be negotiable. If a house is new on to the market, normally there is less scope for bargaining.

2 Have there been any other offers? Has a surveyor looked at the house for any party? If there have been offers why have they not been accepted? If a survey has been undertaken why has the sale not proceeded?

What you want to know here, is whether the house has

been down-valued and if so what are its defects? A survey is a bit like taking an expert with you to buy a second-hand car – it might look all right to you, but your companion will soon tell you if there is anything seriously wrong that you should know about.

3 How long have the sellers lived there? Why are they moving? Again, this question will help to disclose if there is anything untoward. Here you should ask what the neighbours are like; find out their ages (e.g., young, middle-aged) and habits.

4 Have the sellers got somewhere to move to? This crucial question needs to be asked before you start going to the expense of surveys and the like. Many sales fall through because sellers change their minds. If this happens after you have incurred costs you might consider playing on the sellers' conscience by asking him to reimburse your costs. Ask the estate agent the questions mentioned above. It is a *most important point* to make that a vendor may not necessarily tell the truth, whereas an estate agent, as a professional, *must not tell lies or deliberately mislead.*

However, the agent is under no obligation to comment say on the structural condition of a house. He is likely to advise you to commission your own survey. That said, it makes sense to keep a note of the questions you ask the estate agent and his answers. Then, should you be aggrieved or misled in any way, you can take the matter up with your solicitor.

When you ask questions of estate agents they *must* answer truthfully and honestly. The Property Misdescriptions Act makes it a criminal offence for an estate agent or anyone else professionally marketing property, including builders (but not private sellers), to give a false or misleading description of a property to a material degree. Property must be accurately described and this requirement extends beyond house particulars. It embraces plans, photographs and comments – including answers to questions – that the agent may make.

When and how much do you offer?

Once you have viewed a house, carefully considered the items in the viewing checklist and had a second visit, you need to consider your offer. If the seller is using an estate agent it is advisable to carry out your negotiations through the agent but be careful not to give too much away.

If you are selling your house as well you could

consider asking your own estate agent to negotiate with the seller's agent on your behalf.

In property deals always remember that there is often flexibility and the range of possibilities can be very wide so good negotiating is important.

Consider a seller's asking price to be just that, an 'asking' price. How flexible a seller is likely to be will depend on a number of factors, including his own personal circumstances, whether he has a property in mind and, very importantly, the state of the property market. For further information see Part 2 – Selling Your Home.

Providing your offer is not so ridiculously low as to offend a seller, consider offering low – after all you can always go up. Your saving could be thousands of pounds!

You should be able to decide what is a fair offer by looking at similar properties that are on the market.

The housing market

There are two extreme conditions the housing market experiences: a boom or a depression. You need to be aware of the state of the housing market, both nationally and especially within the area in which you intend to buy your home. Buying at the right time is crucial to saving money and ultimately, should you eventually sell, to making a profit.

In a booming residential property market, houses and flats are in short supply and demand is fierce. This causes prices to rise.

Boom conditions lead to 'gazumping', where a seller having already accepted a bid from one buyer, accepts a higher bid from a different buyer. In such a market you will have to make up your mind more quickly whether or not you want to buy a particular property. Furthermore, it will not be so easy to reduce the asking price for a property because the vendor will be confident of achieving a sale even if he refuses your bid. He will expect to receive his asking price or a figure very close to it.

In a depressed housing market, there will be a large number of houses for sale and prices may actually be falling. If such market conditions coincide with high interest rates, as they did in 1989–90, you, as a buyer, will tend not to 'push yourself' for a mortgage to the same extent. At the same time, bargain-basement prices will be the order of the day and, over both the short- and long-term, considerable savings can be made through buying now. If you are a first-time buyer or have already sold your existing home, you will be placed in a strong negotiating position to take full advantage of the opportunities available.

CASE STUDY

In a very slow-moving market, one typical couple had sold their own house and were living in rented accommodation. They were looking at a recently completed estate where a small four-bedroomed detached house was selling for around £90,000.

They went to view a number of similar houses and put down offers of around £80,000. Most owners indignantly refused the offer out of hand, but one vendor, anxious for a sale, agreed to sell their house for £80,000 on condition that the sale went through very quickly. The moral of this story is, be persistent and you may strike gold.

There are many other examples of large reductions in price, like the pop star in London who dropped his price by £500,000 in order to get a quick sale.

How you can find out what is happening in the housing market

The 'market' varies from one part of the country to another and there can be different trends in towns close to one another. It isn't sufficient, therefore, simply to read your national newspaper as this could be misleading. It could be that property prices generally are depressed but have held up remarkably well in your vicinity. Moreover, within your area, there will be parts that hold the value of property better than others.

You'll need to talk to local professional people including estate agents, building society managers and solicitors, to ascertain what exactly is happening in specific locations.

Comb your national and local press for features on property. The map on page 20 shows the 11 standard regions in Britain.[1] You can get reports from major lending institutions (issued at regular intervals throughout any one year), which break down trends on a regional basis and can therefore give you a broad picture of what is happening to property prices in your particular region.

Reports from the Halifax and Nationwide are available free on the Internet.

Alternatively you may be able to obtain the reports from your local branch of some financial institutions.

As previously stated however, bear in mind that the reports can often

---

[1] If you are interested in going into further depth, you can read the following reports, but be warned not to take them as gospel truth.

THE STANDARD UNITED KINGDOM
HOUSING REGIONS

SCOTLAND

NORTHERN
IRELAND

NORTH

ISLE OF MAN

YORKSHIRE &
HUMBERSIDE

NORTH
WEST

EAST
MIDLANDS

WEST
MIDLANDS

EAST ANGLIA

WALES

SOUTH
EAST

SOUTH WEST

contradict one another. The Royal Institution of Chartered Surveyors deliberately avoids complicated analysis. Instead, its periodic reports record the impressions of its members on the way house prices are moving in different categories of property.

You may well find that good estate agents are perhaps best able to advise on the state of their patch. This may or may not correspond to the national trend. Indeed, it's quite possible for a locality to defy regional as well as national trends, especially if it has unusual characteristics which make it an especially desirable place to live and one where demand always exceeds supply.

Location, location, location

Property is always about location. The golden rule is to select an area where the best properties are available. In simple terms, property is the most valuable where the most wealth already exists or is in the process of being created.

In many towns and cities there will be an acknowledged 'good' area or areas, usually within the outer suburbs. The same principle also applies to villages.

Good transport and amenities, including schools, libraries and so on, are also important.

You should locate your home in as good an area as you can afford (the better the area the higher property prices tend to become). If at all possible, avoid choosing a home which is within or close to a recognised 'downmarket' area. Even if it is a perfectly good house in itself, it will not appreciate in value to anything like the same extent as a similar property in a more congenial location and in real terms its worth could actually plummet.

> Remember – certain property types do generally have ceiling figures. For instance, a terraced house or a semi-detached property may not increase in value much above the usual price for them, no matter what their location.

A danger to be aware of for many people investing in their own home is that they either over-improve the building or spend money on renovations that do not add any value, like stone cladding on the walls. It is a good tip for you to buy an over-improved property at the 'right' price if you can find one.

Similarly, a neglected property in the 'right' area can also be a very good buy indeed. An example might be a property possessed by a bank or building society.

It is possible that some locations are set to improve over

time and prices in such locations will rise accordingly. Some residential areas in cities become more fashionable whilst others lose their attraction. It could be beneficial if you were able to ascertain those improving areas, because it is then likely that your home will rise significantly in value within a few years.

Things to look for are: a lack of vandalism; good pubs; nicely presented shops, etc.

There are a number of tell-tale signs to look for which can increase the appeal of a location. One is transport. For example, if a new motorway or major motorway feeder road is to be built, then the value of proximate localities often shoots up. Don't wait for the motorway to be constructed but, if possible, buy in the planning stage or the bargains will have gone. Do make sure however, that you know exactly where the new motorway and its feeder roads are to run. You will want to avoid buying in a quiet residential street, only to find it becomes noisy and busy later on. Other possible pointers are discussed below.

The condition of an area is important when you come to sell your house in the future. Look closely at the local shops and facilities and actually visit them to gain a first-hand impression. Make enquiries at the local library as to what organisations exist and generally get to know the surrounding area before you buy.

If all this sounds too time-consuming, remember you are making a vitally important decision and you must make it carefully.

In buying a house in haste you could well repent at leisure.

WHAT MAKES A GOOD LOCATION?

We have looked in general at what makes a good location. Now let us consider what to look for in more detail.

1 Schools

Whether you have children or not, it is important to understand the link between good schools and selling houses. If your property happens to be close to a school with a bad reputation then this is a definite minus. On the other hand, if your home is within the catchment area of a respected school, then you will find that this is a positive selling point and drawing feature. Such a location can add as much as 5 per cent to the property value.

2 Shops and Pubs

Shops and pubs need to be within convenient walking or commuting distance. A few minutes' walking distance is ideal, or else five or ten minutes by car. The golden rule is that such facilities should not be on your doorstep. Such a situation will inevitably create noise by day and night and put people off buying.

3 Open View

An attractive outlook is an important consideration when assessing location. Here the situation is similar to the seaside resort hotel. Those on the front, offering sea views, are able to charge the most. Views over countryside and/or water are especially attractive and are most likely to be found in green areas. For city and town dwellings, residents often have to make do with man-made views – golf courses, parks and open spaces – and while not being as good as authentic countryside are much preferable to seeing other houses in all directions. In fact, views over chimney stacks and electricity pylons could lose over 15 per cent of a property's value.

4 Orientation

The direction in which your house faces can be important. Britain is a nation of keen gardeners and sun-worshippers, for which reason many buyers, including perhaps yourself, look for rear gardens with a southerly aspect.

5 Transport Facilities

Country houses close to motorway networks and airports can command a good premium. In major cities, proximity to important railway facilities can also add value to a property. Good bus routes can also be important. On the other hand,

if you are too close to a motorway or railway and can't escape from their noise, your property will fall in value and will prove difficult to sell. For instance, estate agents have found it extremely difficult to sell properties on the direct line of the rail link to the Channel Tunnel.

6 Seclusion and Tranquility

A property in a scenic village, within a few minutes of main rail and motoway networks, can be very attractive, but so too can a house in a quiet road in a town or city. A similar property on a major road, on the other hand, will often be worth much less than a residence connecting into it via a minor feeder road, tucked conveniently away from the hustle and bustle of the traffic-infested route.

7 Good Sporting and Leisure Facilities

Houses located within easy reach of good leisure or sporting facilities will often be in greater demand than similar properties situated elsewhere. There are over two thousand golf courses in England and Wales alone, and their number is still increasing. A house overlooking a golf course will be much coveted by golfing enthusiasts, as well as those keen on the pleasant view and relatively low risk of new housing developments appearing. A local leisure centre at a convenient distance will also be a plus.

Houses to avoid buying

When buying a house it is important to ask the question: Will the house readily sell in the future? It is a fact that some houses sell easily whilst others can prove extremely difficult to sell. It is a grave mistake not to consider selling when buying. Even if you don't believe you will move and are convinced you've found your 'dream' home, your circumstances could change, compelling a future sale. You therefore need to select a property that will at least retain its value and ideally will increase in value over the coming years. You should look carefully at the following points:

• Try to avoid buying a house in a very poor or deteriorating location. Even if your home is a palace its value will be held down if it adjoins or is near to very neglected properties;

• Beware of homes with specific drawbacks where too many people will impose on privacy. Examples include:
busy bus stops;
football grounds;
bottle banks;
public houses; and
children's play areas;

• Beware too of houses which fall directly beneath a main flight path to a busy airport as these can also be difficult to sell;

• Avoid if possible houses near to commercial premises such as:
factories;
abattoirs;
funeral parlours;
noisy discos, and the like;

• Note also that poorly designed houses, both in external appearance and with difficult internal arrangements will become a liability rather than an asset to their owner. For instance, having to get to one bedroom through another, a cramped and inadequate bathroom and similar drawbacks. Nothing looks more out of place today than the 'ultra-modern' properties of the late 1960s and early 1970s.

Generally it is sound advice to avoid buying non-traditional houses, such as system-built ones made with concrete and steel. Many banks and building societies refuse to lend on such housing types anyway.

The main types of home

TERRACED HOUSES

The benefit of terraced houses is that they tend to be cheaper than semi-detached or detached properties. They therefore often make excellent homes for first-time buyers.

As with flats, noisy neighbours can be a nuisance. If

your neighbour has a problem, you will soon get to hear about it! Another common drawback is the general lack of on-site car parking and garages.

External improvements must be kept in character with neighbouring terraced houses which restricts individuality.

SEMI-DETACHED HOUSES

The main drawback with semi-detached houses is their closeness to neighbouring properties, an inevitable consequence of their side-to-side arrangement. At the same time, not all neighbours are inconsiderate and, unlike terraced houses, you'll only be joined to one other residence. Semi-detached houses also have a more modern and attractive appearance than terraced properties and will often include garage facilities, especially if they are part of a purpose-built estate.

DETACHED HOUSES

These are often the most expensive type of home, but are probably the best investment. They offer you greater independence in the lifestyle you can lead, with neighbours kept at a distance. Normally detached houses have bigger gardens where you can relax in private. My advice is to go for this type if you can possibly afford it. Remember, though, to ensure that it is not surrounded by inferior properties.

BUNGALOWS

A bungalow can either be detached or semi-detached. Bungalows often have great appeal for older people who like the fact that there are no stairs to climb. Maintenance is often easier. More and more people are living longer and, for the retired, bungalows are likely to remain a very popular type of home. They are also very suitable for couples who have no children living at home, or for single people who don't need as much room as a family. The drawback of bungalows is obviously that there are fewer rooms available than in a comparable two-storeyed house.

COUNTRY COTTAGES

Country cottages are akin to works of art – they tend to hold their value. Their attraction derives from the rural setting in which they are found – often in an isolated spot or quiet village. As such they are very popular with city dwellers who use them as weekend retreats. Where they act as principal residences, they can have their drawbacks, especially in winter when heating bills will often be more expensive than in modern houses. There is the possibility of the house being cut off should there be heavy snowfalls and the difficulty of using the local roads which can be treacherous in icy conditions.

FLATS

Most of the material in this book holds good for a flat as well as a house. However, if you are contemplating buying a flat, then there are some specific points applicable to this type of property that you need to be aware of:

• Flats are either purpose-built, that is designed to be a flat, or else are converted from a larger, old house which then forms several flats. In the latter case, you need to be satisfied that the whole building, including roof and gutters, is in good condition, and that services, such as electricity and water, are totally separate from other flats in the converted building. After all, you only want to be paying your own bills!

• Another factor to bear in mind when buying a flat is that the legal fees may be higher than for a house of a similar value. This is because there is more work involved for the solicitor in checking out matters connected with the lease.

• The vast majority of flats are sold leasehold and many lending institutions will only lend money where leasehold is available and there are satisfactory arrangements for the maintenance and repair of the building.

• It follows that when buying a flat your solicitor will have to consider carefully the lease details and what provision is made for ongoing maintenance (roof, drains etc.) and how the common parts (stairs, halls, gardens, etc.) are to be maintained in terms of cleaning, decorating, and gardening.

• One drawback with flats is the maintenance and service charges. These can often be very expensive and it is wise to bear in mind that each year the charges are more likely to go up than down.

• It is advisable not to consider buying a flat with less than about 70 years to run on the lease, otherwise buyers and lending institutions become very wary. Indeed, where there is less than around 45 years to run it is unlikely that a mortgage can be obtained, so a cash purchase will probably be required.

• Bear in mind also that noisy neighbours (and even the quietest can be obtrusive given that you will literally be living on top of each other) can be a nuisance. This applies especially where sound insulation is not good.

• Finally, there are many benefits from living in a flat. Like bungalows, being all on one level makes them easier to clean than a house. Many people feel safer living in a flat especially if it is not on the ground floor and it has the benefit of a door entry alarm system. Further, there is often no exterior maintenance or gardening to do.

Current leasehold legislation

By 1993, 750,000 people in the UK lived in leasehold flats. In 1993 the Leasehold Reform, Housing and Urban Development Act gave certain qualifying flat owners the ability either to extend their leases indefinitely or to buy their underlying freehold. This is a somewhat limited market covering London and other pockets of leasehold property.

In the longer term, the main benefits of the Act should be that conveyancing of leasehold property may be made simpler and the value of a flat will not dwindle away at the end of a lease.

There are a number of qualifications you must have to buy your freehold e.g., at least half the leaseholders in a block must have occupied their flats for the past twelve months or three of the past ten years etc.

The Leasehold Enfranchisement Advisory Service (see page 156) provides free advice and maintains lists of valuers and solicitors who can provide help in what is a fairly specialist and complex area.

When to buy

For first-time buyers, a case can be made out for renting in the first instance before moving on to home ownership. This would apply more in a slow or static market place, where first-time buyers can afford the *time* to rent whilst looking around for a good deal. However, in a time of sustained rising prices it may be best to get on the housing ladder as quickly as possible, at whatever cost.

The best time to consider buying a house is when you have maximum choice. In normal market conditions this can often be during the winter months, between November and February, when the least number of buyers are around and fewer houses are selling. You will see a property and its garden (if any) at their worst during this time, which has the advantage of letting you know exactly what you are taking on. For the same reasons, even in good market conditions, the winter can still be a good time to buy. When the market is moving slowly and there is a considerable choice of houses available for sale, you may be able to pick up a bargain.

The absolutely ideal time to buy in reality probably never comes along. The time for you to look will be determined by your individual circumstances.

The typical costs of buying a house

1
LEGAL COSTS
(see Chapter 2)

(a) Stamp Duty (currently starting at 1 per cent of house purchase price over £60,000)
(b) Local Search(s)
(c) Land Registry Fees
(d) Solicitor's Disbursements
(e) Solicitor's Fee*
(f) Lending Source's Legal Fees*

2
FINANCIAL/MORTGAGE COSTS
(see Chapter 3)

(a) Mortgage indemnity guarantee (if applicable)*
(b) Building insurance*
(c) Contents insurance*
(d) Removal fees (if applicable)*
(e) Early redemption fee*
(f) Interest payments*

3
THE VALUATION AND SURVEY
(see Chapter 4)

(a) Lender's Valuation and Report
(b) HSV or Building Survey Fee*

Don't forget, some of the above costs will also incur VAT.

*Costs which are not necessarily fixed or else are open to negotiation. These are covered in detail in the relevant sections of the book.

THE LEGAL ASPECTS

THE LEGAL ASPECTS

The legal side of buying your home: key money-saving points

1 Always negotiate or shop around on legal fees. You can easily save hundreds of pounds for your efforts.

2 Ensure you know what you will have to pay if your purchase falls through for any reason or there are other complications.

3 Be clear on exactly what is included in your fee by asking for a quotation in writing clearly breaking down Search Fees, VAT, etc.

4 Save money by doing your own conveyancing – but make sure you have a thorough grasp of exactly what is involved.

5 Save money by using the same solicitor as your mortgage lender.

How do you choose your solicitor?

Choosing a solicitor is not necessarily easy. Although cost is an important factor, above all else you want someone who will do a good job for you. Speed is vital because delay at any stage could result in you losing the property you want. Hence the importance of your solicitor keeping in touch with you on a regular basis.

In selecting a solicitor you could act on a recommendation from friends or professionals you may come across when setting out to buy your new property, such as an estate agent or a building society manager.

Ideally, you want to be dealing with a specialist conveyancing solicitor. Some solicitors take on a wide variety of legal work. This is good in one sense, but in practical terms can mean that when you want to contact the solicitor he is out at court and unavailable, a major drawback when rapid action is required.

Conveyancing can be

routine work, but try to ensure that a qualified solicitor or an experienced legal executive rather than a junior articled clerk is responsible for most of your legal work.

House sales can fall through for many reasons. Many may not be your fault. For example, a buyer further down the chain may pull out or the person selling the house may decide not to move. You should check with your solicitor in advance what he would do regarding charging you in such an eventuality. If you find an alternative property and proceed with the move, many solicitors only charge a nominal additional amount on their fee, but of course you will have to pay for any searches, etc, that they have already completed on your behalf.

First steps

By the time you have found a house you wish to buy, you should have obtained a few quotations from solicitors and decided which of them you will be employing. You should also have decided on the building society or bank you will be using, and the amount and type of mortgage you will be having (see Chapter 3).

Your solicitor will try to find out everything about the property you intend to buy and will request a draft contract from the seller's solicitor. The contract describes the property, the price agreed, whether the property is freehold or leasehold, and whether there are any restrictions on the use of the property.

The contract shows whether there are any restrictive covenants or easements affecting the property. For instance, are you allowed to put washing on the line on a Sunday? Is there a right of way running through the land? The draft contract will be reviewed over the next few days or weeks until you and the seller are happy with it.

A guide to your solicitor's procedure

Sale

Instructions from you.

Obtain your title deeds.

Prepare sale contract.
Send contracts to purchaser's

Purchase

Instructions from you.

Obtain contract from vendor's solicitor.

solicitors.

Take your instructions,
answer enquiries and send you
a copy.

Contact you to sign when
purchaser's solicitors can
exchange.

Exchange contracts (to be
synchronised if sale and
purchase) and agree completion
date.

Approve sale deed from purchaser's solicitors and answer
any queries on title. Obtain
repayment figure from your
Mortgagees.

Complete sale, pay off mortgage
and account to you.

Raise enquiries on contract and
send off Local Search.

Receive Local Search.

Receive notification from you of
mortgage offer and agree
completion date.

Exchange contracts (to be
synchronised if sale and
purchase).

Check title, raise any purchase
queries and send draft deed
to vendor's solicitors.

Conduct final searches.

Receive replies to enquiries
on title and approve deed.

Send Mortgage Deed to you for
signature and deed to
vendor's solicitors. Apply
for mortgage cheque.

Complete purchase and
formalities and account to you.

Preliminary enquiries

Your solicitor will send out a
standard questionnaire to the
seller's solicitor which will ask
for certain information. This
will include such items as
determining who is responsible
for the boundaries of the property, whether there have been
any problems with the residence, and what fixtures and
fittings will be left behind or be
removed.

The local search

At the same time as raising preliminary enquiries, your solicitor will undertake a local
search on the property you
want to buy. This involves sending a standard form to the local
authority. This will seek to find
out whether there are any proposed development schemes
affecting the area in which the

house is located. It also covers such points as whether there are likely to be road-widening schemes, planning permissions, rights of way – in short, any matter that will affect the property directly or indirectly.

Replies to all these enquiries will be given in writing by the local authority. As with other functions of local government, local residents have to take their turn in being dealt with and sometimes the process can take two to three weeks to complete.

A fee is charged for the local search. This will be incorporated into your solicitor's overall charge.

Mortgage offer/arrangement of finance

While the legal work referred to is proceeding, your lending institution will have arranged for the house you want to purchase to be valued. Even if you are not having a mortgage, it is still important that a survey is carried out during the early stages of the legal work.

If the survey or valuation shows up any problems it is important that you renegotiate the price of the property at this stage.

Should you require a mortgage then your solicitor will satisfy himself that you have a reasonable mortgage offer before going ahead and exchanging contracts.

Chapter 3 will give you more information on mortgages and other financial matters, and Chapter 4 explains the ins and outs of valuations and surveys.

Legal charges on arranging a mortgage

Assuming that your solicitor is also acting for the mortgage lender, they will need to prepare a mortgage deed which forms the legal contract between the lender and you as the buyer.

The level of costs often depends on the size of your mortgage loan. Most lenders will use your solicitor to do the legal work on their behalf, which saves you money, but check this first.

Although legal fees vary nationwide, the following table gives a rough estimate of how much you will be asked to pay for your solicitor's services and other outgoings such as stamp duty on your purchase.

ESTIMATE OF LEGAL CHARGES

Legal fees on a sale at £55,000	£ 400
VAT	£ 70
Legal charges on purchase at £100,000	£ 360
VAT	£ 63
Stamp Duty	£1,000
Land Registry Fee	£ 200
Bank Transfer Fee	£ 20
Land Search	£ 44
	£2,157

Solicitors' fees can vary considerably as you will be able to see from the table below. This exercise was carried out over a wide area. It shows how important it is to shop around for a good deal, wherever you live.

CITY LEGAL FEES QUOTED ON A HOUSE PURCHASE AT £100,000

	Solicitor A £	Solicitor B £	Solicitor C £
Birmingham	515	180	350
Bristol	360	320	420
Southampton	320	355	400

N.B. All plus VAT and disbursements

Contract races

If a seller has a number of buyers wanting to acquire the property, it is possible that he will instruct his solicitor to send out more than one contract with the stipulation that the first party to exchange contracts has the property.

From a buying angle, contract races are bad news. You may go for a property and be in a state of high anxiety only to learn that you have lost out. This will be all the more regrettable if legal fees and survey costs may have been incurred.

My advice would be not to get involved in a contract race unless you and your solicitor are happy you can move very quickly and are prepared to accept the fact that you could end up losing the contract race.

If you find yourself drawn into a contract race, sit down with your solicitor. The very fact that a race is on indicates that a property may be going at a bargain price. Whether you will win the race will be very much down to the speed of your solicitor. The attitude he has to adopt is that he is in the race for himself so that all the stops are pulled out.

If you feel you have a bargain property you may also wish for the legal work to go through in double-quick time. In such cases, the saving on the legal fee may be a secondary consideration so it may be worth paying your solicitor more to get the higher (quicker) level of service you want.

The seller's solicitor should advise all the interested parties that a contract race is on. Often this has the effect of all but the most determined dropping out. You could even find that you are the sole purchaser.

Gazumping

Gazumping is when a vendor gives a verbal agreement to accept your offer, but then takes a higher offer before the exchange of contracts. In England and Wales gazumping is not illegal, and is common in a rapidly rising market where housing demand is buoyant. Unfortunately there is not a lot you can do about it.

As a buyer, once you have agreed to buy a property it is important that you complete the buying formalities and exchange contracts as soon as possible. This really is the only way to avoid being gazumped

Existing estate agency practice can compound the problem in as much as estate agents are duty-bound to try to obtain the best possible price for a particular property. They are, after all, employed by the vendor. They are obliged to pass on all offers to the vendor even after a price has been agreed.

If you have acted honourably and done all in your power to buy a property but then find that the vendor is tempted by a higher offer, you could try to play on the vendor's conscience through mentioning the trouble and expense you have gone to, even asking them to reimburse your costs.

Effectively, this is a last resort and it very much depends on the character of the vendor as to whether it will work.

Lock-out agreements

Lock-out agreements became popular especially in London in the mid 1990s. This type of agreement is very attractive for a purchaser who does not wish to be gazumped. Basically vendor and purchaser sign an agreement before exchange of contracts. The vendor agrees not to allow viewers to look at his property within an agreed time span, while the purchaser agrees to exchange contracts by a given date. A criticism of lock-out agreements from a seller's angle is that time can be wasted if the purchaser is unable to proceed for any reason during the time of the agreement (normally two to three weeks).

Exchange of contracts

Once both sides are happy with the contract, the searches and pre-contract enquiries have been completed and your solicitor is satisfied you have received a mortgage offer, then the contracts can be exchanged. At this stage the sale becomes legally binding, a deposit is paid (held by the vendor's solicitor), a completion date is fixed and you no longer have the option to withdraw. The deposit is usually fixed at around 10 per cent of the purchase price, but can be lower.

On exchange of contracts you become liable for the insurance of the property you are buying. If you are having a mortgage, the lender will insist that the property is insured and often will arrange the cover and pay the first premium, deducting this from the amount you receive when the loan is completed.

> If you are selling a property as well as buying one, it is important that the exchange on both sale and purchase takes place simultaneously. Thereby you avoid being committed to a purchase yet still exposed to the danger that the sale of your existing property could fall through. Your solicitor will oversee and co-ordinate this operation.

Investigation of title

Once contracts have been exchanged, but before completion, your solicitor has to investigate the title. He will check the old conveyances to make sure that the person selling actually owns the property. If the property is registered, then the necessary information can easily be obtained from the Land Registry by sending a search form. If the property is leasehold the solicitor checks the lease.

Where the property is not registered, the solicitor has to check all previous transactions concerning the title over the last 15 years.

Compulsory registration came into force in the UK at different times in different places, for instance, 1957 in Leicester and 1975 in Southampton. Your solicitor will find out for you if your new property is unregistered, but if you are doing your own con-veyancing you will need to contact the Land Registry yourself.

Registered and unregistered land

Where a property is registered, you, as a buyer, can obtain all the information about ownership of the property from the Land Registry. Not all land is registered, but in areas where reportage is compulsory a property then either has a registered title, or when the house is next sold, the title has to be registered by the new owner.

More work is involved in confirming the true title to a particular plot of land if it is not registered and the cost incurred by your solicitor in this respect could be added onto your bill.

The conveyance or transfer deed document

This is the deed that passes the seller's interest in the property to you, the buyer. A draft of this is sent after exchange of contracts to the seller's solicitor for approval. Once he has given his endorsement, your solicitor will engross (prepare) the final version of the deed. At this stage he also asks you for the balance of the purchase money. If you are having a mortgage he has to sign the Mortgage Deed.

Your solicitor (who will usually also be acting for your mortgage lender) will then apply for the mortgage cheque.

If the reply to any further searches is satisfactory and the mortgage monies are available, you and the vendor will make arrangements for completion. This is the time that you take possession of the property and your solicitor receives the Title Deeds in exchange for the balance of the purchase price.

Your solicitor ensures that any outstanding mortgage on the property you are buying is paid off and normally gives a bankers' draft for the balance in exchange for the conveyance signed by the seller.

How long does all this take?

Because no house is the same and each person's circumstances are different, the completion of the legal process of buying a house can vary considerably. Assuming there is no chain and no problems, from the time your solicitor is notified and the conveyancing procedure starts, exchange of contracts will usually occur after about six to eight weeks.

Completion can take place within a few days or weeks of this.

If on the other hand you are caught in a chain, you may find it taking three to four months for everyone to get sorted out.

After completion

Your solicitor will have the conveyance stamped by the Inland Revenue. At this stage the Stamp Duty is paid if applicable (see page 39).

The transaction now has to be registered at the Land Registry. It can often be several months before this takes effect. After this legal formality has been completed, your solicitor will either give the deeds to you, if you are not having a mortgage, or to your lender if you are.

Land registry fees

When you are buying a house Land Registry Fees must be paid for either registering the title to the house if it has not been previously registered, or for registering the transfer of the title to the house where it has already been registered.

Value or amount (£)			Fee (£)
0	–	40,000	40
40,001	–	70,000	70
70,001	–	100,000	100
100,001	–	200,000	200
200,001	–	500,000	300
500,001	–	1,000,000	500
1,000,001 and over			800

Stamp duty

Stamp Duty is a government tax payable only on the purchase of a house or flat. Normally it isn't payable for dwellings at the cheaper end of the market, though the exact point at which it applies will vary. (Currently 1 per cent starting at £60,000.)

It may be possible to save paying the cost of the Stamp Duty. More accurately it might be feasible to get the seller of the property to pay this for you.

In certain market conditions, as a marketing ploy, many estate agents may advertise property with the slogan 'Stamp Duty paid by the seller'. Be careful, however, to ensure that you have negotiated a good price in the first place. There is little point in saving £600 worth of stamp duty if you could have negotiated a further £1000 off the asking price.

Licensed conveyancers

Licensed conveyancers are specialist lawyers trained and qualified in the legal processes needed to deal with the transfer of residential property.

The profession was created by an Act of Parliament in 1985 specifically to compete with solicitors for conveyancing work.

Licensed conveyancers have to comply with various rules of practice laid down by the profession's regulatory body, the Council for Licensed Conveyancers. They must have insurance against any liability arising from errors or omissions, so they are able to offer

the same quality of protection to you as their client as that provided by solicitors.

A list of licensed conveyancers operating in England and Wales can be obtained from the Society of Licensed Conveyancers (see page 134).

A complaint against licensed conveyancers is that some only deal with clients by post and are reluctant to come to the telephone. A further disadvantage is that they may not be able to process the legal work for lenders so a solicitor will still have to be appointed and paid to do this. Check on this point.

Doing your own conveyancing

The attraction of DIY conveyancing is naturally that you can save money. Be warned though that if you are buying a property with a mortgage, the

saving involved in DIY conveyancing may not be that great. Indeed, you will still have to pay the lender's solicitor's charges.

There are a number of books that take you step-by-step through the process: the *Which? Guide to Conveyancing* or R.T. Steel's *DIY Conveyancing*. Ensure that you obtain the most up-to-date editions of these publications.

Even so, it's a bit like driving through London with the aid of an AA route guide – possible but teeming with problems. Where in the capital you're liable to end up in a traffic jam which will hold up your progress, with DIY conveyancing you will have to do all the paperwork normally handled by a solicitor. For someone inexperienced, this will take time – usually considerably longer than a solicitor even if you do avoid the fees. You will also need easy access to a typewriter (or word processor) and photocopier.

Be warned at the outset: there are a lot of things to consider and mistakes can be costly.

We have briefly looked at what is legally involved when buying a house, but to give you a detailed breakdown it would take up the rest of this book! For instance, you will need to investigate whether the seller has the right to sell the property. This can only be resolved by checking the title deeds or the Office Copy Entries from the Land Registry.

Another fundamental issue to be settled is whether there are outstanding charges or loans on the property. If so, these must be cleared by the time you buy or the lending institution could still have an interest in the property you have bought!

If you are selling as well as buying you are likely to be involved in a chain and your sale and purchase should reach the same stage simultaneously.

Remember, too, that if you do your own conveyancing you will only save on the solicitor's charges and the VAT on these. Stamp Duty, Local Searches, Land Registry Fees, etc. will still have to be paid. You are breaking the law if you fail to register your ownership and putting matters right can be very expensive.

If you require a mortgage, your lender will require a solicitor to act for it to ensure that its interests in the property are protected. Even if you do your own conveyancing, therefore, you will still be landed with some solicitors' costs – in this case their fee for acting on behalf of the lender.

When not to do your own conveyancing

Think very carefully about doing your own conveyancing in the following situations:

1 Where you are a first-time buyer with no previous experience of moving.

2 Where the property is leasehold. Understanding leases and the implications of covenants in them can be difficult.

3 When buying an unregistered house in what is now a compulsory registration area. In this case you will have to make the first registration which is more involved than the registration of a transfer.

4 When buying or selling in Scotland. The law is different in Scotland (see page 42), and is inclined to be more complicated.

Another factor to consider is that if a solicitor makes a mistake you may have a case and be able to claim for damages.

On the other hand, a mistake made by you as a DIY conveyancer will only affect you. There can be no legal redress and no one to blame but yourself.

If you do decide to do your own conveyancing, proceed with caution. Read the recommended literature carefully and, if you know anyone who has successfully completed their own conveyancing, seek their advice.

Case study

A person was desperate to buy a house and the market was moving rapidly. Prices were going up daily.

The gentleman concerned had managed to sell his own house and had to exchange contracts on a new house in the course of construction.

He was selling through a reputable firm of solicitors and reminded his solicitor that he had to exchange contracts on his house sale and on the purchase of the new house on a particular day.

Despite this reminder, the solicitor failed to carry out the instructions and as a result the builders took immediate advantage and increased the new house's price by £50,000. My associate was not able to afford the new asking price, as a consequence of which the property was sold to another buyer.

It took some time, but the gentleman received damages of £50,000 from his solicitor.

Once again, this rams home the key point that if you attempt to do your own conveyancing and 'overlook' a vital matter you will have no recourse for any compensation.

Buying a house in Scotland

Buying and selling a domestic property in Scotland differs from the system in the rest of Britain. Although there are estate agents *per se* in Scotland many solicitors also take it upon themselves to fulfil this role.

Solicitors can subscribe to solicitors' property centres which keep details of properties provided by a number of solicitors. The centres have information relating to a large amount of property on the market and buyers are welcome to visit them and browse through property details. Property centres do not normally arrange viewing properties, but further particulars can be obtained from the solicitor responsible for the residence in which you are interested.

Perhaps the main difference with the legal procedure in Scotland is that there is no such thing as an offer subject to contract. In the rest of the UK, a buyer or seller can withdraw from a sale up until the point that contracts are exchanged with no penalty whatsoever. In Scotland any written offer (missive of sale) you make becomes binding once it has been accepted in writing.

Mortgage offers and surveys in Scotland

In Scotland you should have your mortgage offer and survey carried out before making an offer.

It is esential that you are sure you can finance the purchase and that the money will be available when required before you submit your bid.

Your lender will only be happy to offer a mortgage when the property has been assessed by a qualified valuer to determine its worth, the price is agreed and the lender is satisfied with the property's condition.

If you were to make an offer without getting the approval of your lender you could find yourself legally committed to buy a house for which you cannot get a loan.

Should you be having a more detailed valuation and report (HSV or Building Survey) it is important this is done prior to making your offer, which should then reflect the valuation and any repairs that the surveyor has highlighted may be necessary.

The offer to purchase

The offer to purchase will be prepared by your solicitor and signed on your behalf. Your solicitor should establish whether anyone else is interested in the property you wish to purchase.

If other parties are interested, a seller may fix a date by which any offers have to be made (see page 44). If the property market is flat and no other parties are interested in the property, then there is more scope for negotiating the price downwards. Sometimes a property will be advertised at a fixed price indicating the seller intends to accept the first offer at this figure.

The conveyance in Scotland

Once an offer has been put forward and accepted, a legally binding contract comes into effect and neither you nor the seller can pull out of the transaction. You also become responsible for insuring the property, a matter which your solicitor should take care of.

The following conveyancing procedure will transfer the legal ownership of the property from the seller to you. Your solicitor will obtain the title deeds from the seller's solicitor. He will study these to ensure that the property is free from defects and draw your attention to any legal conditions affecting the property.

Often the bank or building society will instruct your solicitor to prepare the necessary documents, which will reduce your legal costs. Once your solicitor can confirm that all is satisfactory with the title the loan will be forwarded to him.

Your title in your new home will have to be stamped and will need to be registered in the appropriate property register.

There are two registers. The first is the Register of Sazines. There is no guarantee that a deed registered in this register is valid. This is for your solicitor to clarify.

Since 1979 there has been a new register called the Land Register, and registration of title is gradually being introduced throughout Scotland. Once a title has been recorded in this register the title has the benefit of a statutory guarantee.

The legal costs of buying in Scotland

Your solicitor will include all the preliminary work up to the offer stage, the transfer of the property to you (the conveyance) and dealing with legal work on your loan. Stamp Duty has to be paid in Scotland as elsewhere at the appropriate rate (see page 39).

There are no licensed conveyancers in Scotland but competition has meant that fees vary so ring for quotations.

For instance, as an exercise, enquiries in Edinburgh were made, picking out three solicitors at random. The lowest estimate received for the legal work on a £100,000 purchase was £800, the highest £920 with the middle figure being £870. By consulting just one solicitor, therefore, you could well end up paying more than you need to.

The advantages and disadvantages of buying in Scotland

The main advantage with the Scottish system from a buying viewpoint is that gazumping is virtually eliminated. The absence of chains means that neither buyer nor seller has to worry about matters over which they have no control.

A disadvantage is that there could be wasted expense in the survey because this needs to be carried out before submitting an offer. However, there is often only one party interested in a house and it is possible to make an offer subject to a satisfactory survey being carried out. That way, if the offer is not acceptable, the expense of the survey need not be incurred.

Another disadvantage is the way the system deals with a situation where a number of parties are interested in a property. Here the use of sealed bids (similar to tender in the rest of the UK) means that you may pay considerably more than you need to for a property. Conversely, you might lose out through bidding too low.

Arguably another drawback lies in the fact that it does not create chains of transactions at the contract stage, meaning that there is a risk that a bridging loan could be needed. These are more common in Scotland and add greatly to expenses.

Finally, no matter which solicitor you use in Scotland, you will almost certainly pay more than their equivalent in England and Wales as there is quite a bit more for them to do.

MORTGAGES AND FINANCIAL MATTERS

MORTGAGES AND FINANCIAL MATTERS

Key money-saving points

1 Be sure to shop around for your mortgage. Compare like with like and when considering an endowment or pension mortgage look at past performance – but be aware that a good track record in the past won't necessarily be repeated in the future. Finding an above average performer could save you thousands of pounds.

2 If possible, try to avoid a mortgage indemnity guarantee. If you can't, then shop around as prices will differ. You could save hundreds of pounds.

3 Avoid paying an arrangement fee for your mortgage which could amount to £100 or more.

4 If you are a first-time buyer, try to secure a 'special' lower rate mortgage.

5 You can save a small fortune if you take out a fixed-term mortgage at the right time. Wait until interest rates are low and look set to fall no further or are low and look set to rise.

6 If you hope to pay off your mortgage early or intend to move within a year or two, save money by opting for a mortgage with a nil or small redemption penalty.

7 You can save a considerable sum by shopping around when insuring (reinstatement and contents) your new home.

8 Do not be afraid to switch lenders if a better deal is on offer. A saving of half a percentage point can quickly reduce your costs.

The right mortgage for you

It is surprising how many people devote a considerable amount of time in finding the right house, then don't bother to spend sufficient time over seeking out an appropriate mortgage. At best, the result is that they end up paying much more than they need. At worst, they could find their cherished home possessed.

It is vitally important, therefore, that you take time to consider exactly which type of mortgage you take on. After all, you could be stuck with it for 25 years! A lot is going to depend on your own circumstances and, of course, it is not possible to forecast with precision what is going to happen in the future. You may well get married, start a family, become divorced, you might even die.

If you knew what was going to happen, everything would be much simpler! But life isn't like that and you can only make a decision today based on your current situation and immediate expectations.

It would be easier, too, if there were such a creature as an 'ideal' mortgage.

Unfortunately, all mortgage types have pluses and minuses. A couple with a young family may be better off with the endowment type; a young person buying a flat but who expects to get married in the future may be best suited to a repayment mortgage; a self-employed person in a sound business may be well advised to take out a pension mortgage.

Bear in mind also that lending institutions and profession-al advisers may have a vested interest in you taking out a particular type of mortgage. For example, the commissions paid by insurance and pension companies for endowment and pension mortgages can amount to hundreds of pounds. No commission is payable on repayment mortgages, for which reason these sometimes aren't recommended.

Just make sure that you take out the mortgage that is best for you. As well as reading this section thoroughly, buy one or two of the specialist mortgage magazines to get a totally up-to-date picture of what is available. *Your Mortgage*, for example, provides a monthly picture of best buys and lowest rates in the mortgage field.

If you're still not sure, consult an independent financial adviser from whom you can seek specific and unbiased counsel. Be prepared to pay for your adviser's services. If you are not being charged, then the firm may *not* be 'independent'!

You stand to save thousands of pounds by choosing your mortgage carefully. What's more, you won't have to wait 25 years to see the benefits – the saving will often be apparent after just five years of the mortgage.

How big a mortgage should you have?

A mortgage may be defined as a loan secured on the bricks and mortar (and possibly the land) value of a property.

There are two schools of thought as to how much money you should put down on a house. Mortgages of up to 100 per cent may still be available in certain cases, although they are not as common as they used to be. It is likely, therefore, that some down-payment will be required by the lender.

The benefits of a small down-payment on a property include the fact that you have more money to spend on other items such as furniture and fittings. On the other hand, considering your house as an investment, the more equity you have in it the better. A larger down-payment means a lower mortgage, which results in turn in a lower monthly repayment rate. This is important. The historically high interest rates of the late 1980s hit hardest those people with the biggest mortgages to pay and they ended up paying far more for their houses than those who chose to make a substantial down-payment.

How much can you borrow?

Most lending institutions allow as a minimum two-and-a-half to three times the main salary plus, where applicable, a second salary once over. Therefore, a person earning £20,000 with a partner earning £10,000 may be able to negotiate a mortgage of at least £70,000.

Your own lifestyle will dictate how much money you are prepared to pay out on a mortgage, but be careful not to overstretch yourself too much. You will need spare cash for basic living expenses, even if you don't indulge in luxuries. Allow some leeway in your calculations to allow for rising prices and inflation.

Allow for the fact that interest rates can go up and if, for example, you decide to start a family, or add to your existing one, you may lose the second income for a time, if not permanently.

By filling in the following chart you will be able to see how much cash you have and how much you can afford to pay on a new mortgage.

Income per month	Self Partner Other (e.g. child benefit, interest from savings etc.)	
A. TOTAL INCOME PER MONTH		
Expenditure per month	Council tax Water rates House/Contents insurance Life insurance/Pension Gas/Electric/Other fuel Telephone Car expenses Travelling Credit cards Hire purchase School fees Housekeeping (food/ clothing) Other expenses	
B. TOTAL EXPENDITURE PER MONTH		
Excess of Income over Expenditure = A–B		
Less New Mortgage Payment		
SPARE CASH		

Subject to valuation and subject to status

Whichever mortgage type you opt for, your lender will not advance any money until certain facts have been established to their satisfaction.

Your lender will want a valuation carried out on the property you wish to buy to ensure that it provides adequate security for the loan. The valuation is not a detailed survey (see following section on surveys).

They will also demand confirmation that you can afford to pay your loan and will write to your employer for confirmation of your salary and other details. If you are self-employed, the lender will probably want to inspect trading accounts.

Choosing your mortgage: the types available

Once you have decided to move it is important that you consider the question of the mortgage you will need to buy the house of your choice. Remember that all mortgages involve a degree of risk, but some more so than others.

All mortgages are effectively variants on two themes:

1 With a 'repayment' mortgage, you pay back both interest and capital throughout the term of the agreement.

2 With an 'endowment' type mortgage, you pay interest only over the term of the loan. The capital is paid by means of either an endowment policy, a pension plan, or an individual savings account (ISA).

Let's consider these and other options in more detail.

REPAYMENT MORTGAGE

This type of mortgage, also called an Annuity Mortgage or a Capital and Interest Mortgage, involves paying off the capital borrowed and interest on the remaining debt over the term of the mortgage.

No life assurance is included with this type of mortgage so it is necessary to have some form of mortgage protection so that in the event of death, the outstanding mortgage will be paid off.

A repayment mortgage is a straightforward and flexible mortgage. For example, you can keep repayments at a higher level if interest rates drop and that way reduce the number of years the mortgage has to run. Alternatively, should interest rates rise, you can in some circumstances keep repayments constant and extend the term of the loan.

LOW-COST ENDOWMENT MORTGAGE

There are a number of potential benefits with a low-cost endowment mortgage. They include the provision of life assurance and a potential tax-free surplus at the end of the mortgage.

Unlike a Capital and Interest Mortgage, a Low-cost Endowment Mortgage involves the repayment of interest only to the lender. The capital element of the mortgage is repaid by means of a Low-cost Endowment Policy. This is a special savings-type of life assurance policy that involves the paying of premiums over a number of years – the term of the mortgage. The most common period is 25 years, though shorter policies, say for 10 or 15 years, are also available.

As the person pays into the low-cost endowment policy, each year a bonus is added to the basic sum assured. This is lower than the mortgage amount so as to keep the cost of the policy reasonably low, hence 'Low-cost'.

The borrower has the assurance of knowing that whatever happens there will *always* be sufficient money to repay the mortgage if they were to die during the term of the mortgage.

By the end of the mortgage, the policy ends and a sum of money is paid out. The intention is that this should be more than sufficient to repay the capital borrowed and will possibly leave a tax-free cash surplus for the policy holder. If the policy performs well there is also the possibility of paying off the mortgage early.

A word of warning

Critics of endowment mortgages ascribe their popularity to the hard selling by lenders and financial advisers. It's clearly in their interests to push these rather than repayment mortgages on which no commission is paid. Typically, the first year's premium on an endowment policy is eaten up by commission. Even a £50 a month endowment policy earns the lender on average a £570 commission!

Beware of special offer endowment mortgages being sold as the cheapest option. Often they aren't. Much depends on individual circumstances. A single person with no dependants isn't well advised to go for an endowment mortgage with life cover they don't require. Should they want life cover later on when they have dependants, then buying term assurance could work out much cheaper. Moreover, should the single person marry someone with an endowment policy, it is likely that one of them will have to be surrendered at considerable loss.

Bear in mind, too, that with most endowment mortgages there is no guarantee that the lump sum will necessarily pay off the mortgage and leave a cash-free lump sum. Don't be persuaded by past examples of performance from the 1980s. Then, roaring inflation and a booming stock market and property boom did much to ensure that a substantial lump sum was paid out as well as the loan being paid off. Without galloping inflation, the lump sums aren't likely to look anywhere near as impressive.

Much hangs on the type of endowment selected and the length of the mortgage term. By the 1990s there were fears that many low-cost and unit-linked endowment policies would not produce sufficient returns to pay off the mortgage. These types were not the traditional endowment policies which guaranteed to pay off the mortgage provided a borrower kept up the payments.

An endowment policy can be a poor short-term investment. Should you cash it in early, you may get back very little indeed for your outlay. Endowment mortgages aren't very suitable either as short-term loans, say under 15 years. Unit-linked endowments, directly linked to the stock market, could well under-perform in such a short period, almost certainly meaning that your premiums will have to increase.

You should avoid a non-profit endowment mortgage. While this guarantees to repay your mortgage in full at the end of the term, there is no provision for a surplus no matter how well or badly the insurance company concerned is performing.

Moreover, this type of mortgage is costlier than a conventional repayment loan with term insurance, which also serves the same objective of guaranteeing to pay off the loan.

PENSION MORTGAGE

This is a variation on the low-cost endowment mortgage but instead of a low cost endowment policy being used to repay the capital, a pension plan is used. This will not only repay the loan at retirement, but also provide a useful lump sum of money and a pension.

This type of mortgage is usually available to the self-employed, or to those in non-pensionable employment. It has significant tax advantages so it can often be successfully recommended by your mortgage/financial services consultant. To qualify for a pension mortgage you will find that you usually need to have (or take out) a personal pension plan.

The main advantage of the pension mortgage is that you receive tax relief on the contributions you make to the pension plan. This makes a pension mortgage extremely tax-efficient – particularly attractive for those people with more successful businesses who pay tax in the higher rate band.

You may have to arrange separate life assurance. You could take out special life assurance policies on which you also get tax relief.

The repayment of the capital sum is paid out of the borrower's tax free lump sum taken from the pension arrangement. Up to 25 per cent of the fund can normally be taken as a tax-free lump sum from a personal pension plan. The remaining 75 per cent of the fund available at retirement is used as a single premium to purchase an annuity which will give the policy holder a pension until death.

The main disadvantage with pension mortgages is that they are not very flexible. As their name implies, they represent a long-term commitment on your part. You cannot cash them in early or before you reach the age of 50.

HIGH-RISK MORTGAGE

Mortgages based on equities (shares) or foreign currencies are not recommended unless you can afford to gamble.

An ISA mortgage, based on the performance of selected shares in the stock market, has the attraction of being tax efficient. With compounded annual interest, the potential is there to make a significant tax-efficient windfall as well as paying off the mortgage. But, equally, there is no guaranteed rate of return. A stock market crash will spell disaster. For this type of mortgage, separate life cover will be demanded by the lender which adds to the costs.

A foreign currency mortgage is perhaps the riskiest of all, even though in the right conditions you stand to gain most.

Essentially, you take out a loan in sterling which is then converted into another currency and interest is paid at the resident country's prevailing base lending rate. The advantage is that the selected country's interest rate will be lower than the UKs.

Sticking with one currency risks the foreign country's interest rate climbing higher than theUKs. Managed currency mortgages are a way round this with your mortgage being switched between currencies. But you'll have to pay a hefty fee. What's more, managers sometimes take a percentage for reducing your debt.

Currency fluctuations and the possibility of sterling's devaluation add uncertainty. Where sterling falls against the selected currency, your mortgage repayments will increase accordingly.

FIXED-INTEREST MORTGAGE

The benefit of these loans is that you know exactly what rate you will be paying for the fixed term which is normally between two and five years. At the end of the period you can either negotiate a new fixed rate or move back to a variable rate of interest.

When they have been latched on to at the right time, fixed-rate mortgages have saved borrowers thousands of pounds. The best time to take out such loans is when interest rates are low and look set to fall no further.

Unfortunately, most borrowers tend to think that taking out a fixed-rate mortgage when interest rates are low is not a good idea. What you need to remember is that you are taking out a medium-term loan so that while, in such a situation, variable mortgages might seem more attractive, they won't necessarily remain so over the period of the fixed-rate mortgage. Generally, interest rates tend to fall in the period immediately preceding a general election, for obvious reasons, but they often rebound back upwards once it has taken place.

However, if interest rates fall below your fixed rate and

continue to stay there, you may well find yourself paying over the odds for your mortgage. In such a situation, if you wish to convert back to a variable rate before the fixed term is up, a substantial penalty will normally be incurred. It is therefore essential that you look very closely at what is involved. But even if you do so, it is remarkable how interest rates can change over a five-year period.

Finally, when considering a fixed-rate mortgage offered at a good rate, you must consider the total costs you will face. This means being aware of the hidden costs. These include arrangement fees and the requirement to buy life assurance and other insurances through the lender itself. With these add-ons, what seems like a bargain deal could actually turn out to be considerably more expensive than other lenders' offers. Consider all the elements carefully before you make a decision.

INTEREST-ONLY MORTGAGE

With this type of loan you just pay the interest on the loan each month. Most people link an interest-only scheme with an investment such as an ISA. The capital could be paid off in other ways. For example, if you knew you were going to inherit a house or a substantial amount of money in the future, this type of mortgage could be used.

VARIABLE-RATE MORTGAGE

The payments with the loan vary according to whether interest rates go up or down in the general economy. If rates fall so will the payments on that type of mortgage, and vice versa. These loans are simple and straightforward and so it may be possible to reduce or extend your mortgage term.

DIRECT MORTGAGES

Some lenders 'sell' mortgages over the telephone. Some lenders will try to get applicants to go into a branch office and if you are a first-time buyer this is probably a good thing.

Because some direct lenders do not have an expensive branch network to support, they are prepared to offer lower rates to applicants. Be aware, though, that some direct lenders, however, require a larger deposit than normal – sometimes 25 per cent of the property price.

Direct mortgages are likely to be of most appeal to a more sophisticated home buyer able to put up a considerable deposit and a clear idea of the type of mortgage they require.

Many direct lenders offer free 'phone lines so it is possible to make enquiries from the comfort of your armchair and compare what your 'savings' are likely to be.

Bridging loans

Bridging loans, available from banks and building societies, are short-term loans to bridge the gap when selling and buying another house. It may be you need to move quickly on the home you want to buy and have to exchange contracts or complete on the new house before you do so on your sale.

Be very cautious about taking on a bridging loan. There will probably be a sizeable arrangement fee to pay. The interest rate, too, could be very high.

There are two types of bridging loan: open and closed. An open bridging loan provides the borrower with a loan before they have managed to sell their home. Open bridging loans are more difficult to obtain when the market is depressed – high street banks tend to offer them more than building societies.

I can't emphasise enough

that taking out this type of bridging loan can be ruinous. In a slow market, it's not unheard of for sellers to take two or three years to offload their existing home. However long it takes, during that period you'll probably have to carry the burden of two loans. Where you've paid off your mortgage, then the risk is a lot less – though you'll still be burdening yourself with unnecessary debt.

A closed bridging loan is much less risky. These are only advanced where the parties have exchanged contracts. Should you take out a closed bridging loan, you ought to be able to save money by taking one out with your existing lender. And because they're a much safer form of loan, the closed type often have lower rates than open bridging loans.

First-time buyer mortgage offers

As a first-time buyer, if you take some time shopping around, you could save yourself a substantial sum of money.

To lending institutions you represent a great catch, promising to give them profits over a long period: the length of your mortgage. Therefore, they will virtually fall over themselves to get your business. Indeed, many building societies will offer substantial interest reductions (often 2 per cent or more) which operate over the first two years of a mortgage. At this point, the rate reverts back to the prevailing interest rate of the lending institution.

So the message here is very simple: explore all available lenders' offers before making your choice and you can save a considerable amount. At the same time, don't be deceived by enticing discount rates if you stand to pay more than you would with other mortgage providers once the discount period is over.

The right mortgage for frequent movers

Which is the best type of mortgage if you move house frequently? In this situation repayment mortgages lose their advantages and you stand to pay more over the longer term, particularly in the middle years. By moving every five years or so you'll reduce the debt only marginally. In fact your situation will be equivalent to the pet mouse who steps onto a rolling wheel and can't understand why he never gets anywhere. However, with house prices increasing, your equity is also increasing.

Fixed-mortgages aren't always portable and redemption charges are usually imposed if they are repaid early. Almost certainly you should refrain from taking out a five-year fixed-rate and stick to two-year deals. If you're not certain that you'll remain living in your present home for the period of the fixed-rate mortgage, then you'd do best to look for alternative mortgage types.

Endowment and pension mortgages are more forgiving of frequent movers. They should be portable, though if your new house costs more than your existing mortgage you would need to increase the contributions. Surrender values for endowment mortgages can be low. If you are buying another house, consider transferring the policy to your new home and then topping up with another loan. You might take out a new endowment policy or pension plan to cover the extra sum involved. In many ways this is a better alternative because it leaves unaffected the date your original mortgage matures. Once that happens, your debt will be much reduced.

Be careful to ensure that your new lender is willing to accept your existing pension plan or endowment policy. If they're not, seek out a lender who will. In any event, don't accept advice to cash in your existing endowment policy and start a new one. It simply isn't financially worthwhile.

See page 61 to decide which is the best mortgage for you.

Re-mortgages

Re-mortgaging, or switching mortgages, is not something to be done lightly. You need to take all the costs into account and consider if you'll end up with a net gain which isn't always the case.

First of all, you need to establish what fees the new lender will charge you. Insist that written quotations include transfer charges (where applicable). On top of these, you may be liable to have to pay valuation, legal and land registration fees. There could also be an arrangement fee and a premium for a mortgage indemnity policy.

Next you need to know the extent to which your existing lender will charge you for a transfer. The penalties could include early repayment charges. These could be avoidable if you give two or three months' notice of your intention to switch to another lender.

Then you or your financial adviser will have to work out how long it will take to recover the costs of a move. Generally,

it isn't worth moving unless the savings made wipe out the costs incurred within a year.

Finally, before taking any decisions, be sure to consult with your existing lender. Rather than lose your business, you could find them willing to work out a new mortgage without involving you in the costs of switching. You might be able to extend the term of your mortgage to reduce the interest rate (not applicable with endowment or pension types). Where a discounted mortgage is on offer, establish for how long the discount lasts. If it is for much less than a year then you probably won't recover the transfer costs.

Some lenders are so keen to become involved in the re-mortgage market they are prepared to stand the legal fees and disbursements, survey costs, VAT etc., so it may be very easy to put your case to them and see just what savings you are likely to make. Ask them to work this out for you!

Buildings insurance

From the time you have exchanged contracts on your house you are responsible for insuring it. This means if you failed to do this and the day after contracts were exchanged the house burned down, you would be held accountable.

Your solicitor and building society will offer advice, but it is worth you stopping to consider the amount and nature of insurance cover you require and getting several quotations on the cost.

Basically you will be responsible for the insurance of the bricks and mortar of the house (the reinstatement value) and of its contents. Cover on the latter can vary considerably so make sure that you compare like with like.

The reinstatement value of a property can be much higher than the market value and it is important not to confuse an insurance or reinstatement valuation of a home with an open market valuation.

The reinstatement value includes demolition, architect's fees, legal fees, etc. Many lenders increase the insurance cover each year to take account of inflation.

The insurance field is a competitive business and you can take advantage of this to reduce your costs. Increasingly, West European firms are infiltrating this market, which has prompted several insurers to offer direct sales, eliminating the middleman and cutting their fees.

The majority of the population tend to use their lending institution to arrange their house insurance; very convenient – but also more expensive. You can anticipate paying a hefty commission of around 30 per cent. Expect your building society to try to persuade you to go with them, but there is no obligation to do so. Under the Courts and Legal Services Act 1990, lenders are required by law to allow a free choice on house buildings insurance. Be careful that your building society doesn't direct you towards an intermediary with a tie-in to them. In some instances, lenders might offer special mortgages provided that you take out insurance with them. Weigh your options carefully and probe into exactly where the 'saving' will be.

Though high-street insurance brokers charge less (normally between 15 per cent and 25 per cent of the bill) you could save even more by using a direct sales enterprise such as Royal Bank of Scotland (Direct Line) or the Swiss company Winterthur (Churchill). Increasingly, the competition from these and other newcomers is forcing others to follow suit so a few enquiries on your part should provide several competitive quotes. Should you

arrange your own house building insurance you are liable to
face an approval fee from your
lender of around £25, though

some levy an annual charge.

Check out the insurance
implications before you take
out a mortgage.

Contents insurance

For contents insurance, you
need to choose between indemnity and new-for-old cover. With
the former you insure your
belongings for the amount they
are worth now. With the latter
you insure your belongings for
the amount it would cost to
replace them as new. New for
old is to be recommended even
if it does cost you that little bit
extra for, unfortunately, burglary is a more common occur-
rence than it was some years
ago. There is also the risk of
fire – ensure that you have a
fire warning system installed
and locate fire extinguishers in
several parts of your home.

You must make sure that
you are covered for the full
value of your belongings. If you
under-insure, the insurance
company will probably scale
down the amount it pays out on
any claim you make – or worse
still it might even refuse to pay
anything at all. Where you have
bought costly items, such as

videos, jewellery and dishwash-
ers, it is best to keep the
receipts as proof of purchase
just in case you fall victim to a
burglary.

Many insurers now prefer
packaged policies: these stipu-
late the amount of cover based
on location and the number of
bedrooms. Often these are
good value for money.

Hundreds of pounds can
sometimes be saved on contents insurance through switching to cheaper companies when
it's time for a policy to be
renewed. For instance, you
could try one of the firms
which don't sell through insurance brokers, thereby avoiding
commission.

Finally, if you have taken
steps to ensure that your house
is very secure, with a fitted burglar alarm and perhaps belongs
to a neighbourhood watch
scheme, you might be able to
negotiate a discount.

Mortgage protection policy

This is a relatively cheap way of
arranging life cover so that if
you died during the term of the
mortgage your loan would be
paid off. With an endowment
policy such insurance is built

in, but it is not with a repayment mortgage.

If you opt for a repayment
mortgage, your lender may
wish to arrange this cover for
you and a commission may be

required. The premiums are often paid every month and depend on factors such as your age, whether or not you smoke, your general health, etc. If you are self-employed and a non-pensioner you can get tax relief.

Ensure that you ask for several quotations and compare like with like.

In addition to life assurance, you should consider what will happen to your mortgage payments if you lose your job or fall ill and cannot work.

Payment protection insurance can help cover you against this eventuality and can be discussed in depth with your lender at the time of taking out your mortgage.

Mortgage indemnity guarantee

A mortgage indemnity guarantee is an insurance policy which protects the lending institution should the borrower default on the loan and the resulting sale of the property fails to cover the total debt.

For the vast majority of first-time buyers, and some second-time buyers, a mortgage indemnity guarantee is unavoidable – it is the price that the lending institution insists you pay in order to obtain a mortgage. Normally, it will apply where the amount of the mortgage exceeds a certain percentage of the property's valuation – usually between 75 and 80 per cent. Unless, therefore, you are fortunate enough to be able to make a considerable down-payment on your new home, a mortgage indemnity guarantee will be applied.

Mortgage indemnity guarantees are good business for the lending institutions. Each one they sell earns them commission and it is extremely unlikely that they will disclose

the amount involved even if directly questioned. Generally, however, commission on such policies amounts to between 25 per cent and 35 per cent of the total premium.

That's a hefty percentage. It is often 'hidden' as the premium can legitimately be added to the loan. If you fail to take this into account it means that while you might have picked out the lowest mortgage rate available, the guarantee can wipe out the advantage of, say, 0.25 per cent off the mortgage rate.

An in-depth survey on a £60,000 mortgage showed that house buyers were paying between £240 and £960 indemnity insurance on a 90 per cent advance depending on the lender; £430 to £1200 on a 95 per cent advance; and £2000 to £8000 on a 100 per cent loan.

If you can't escape from incurring a mortgage indemnity guarantee (a few institutions don't insist on them), then you should aim to make large savings by ensuring that your loan is not far above the cut-off point. To achieve this, you could raise an additional sum elsewhere.

Study the following tables carefully. They give a break down of the various types of mortgages available, an explanation of the different interest rates and a guide to their suitability for purchasers.

REPAYMENT METHODS

RATE	DESCRIPTION	SUITABLE FOR
REPAYMENT	Monthly payments are both interest and capital, so that by the end of the agreed term, the loan has been paid off.	People who don't need the extra life insurance offered by an endowment policy, and who want to be absolutely sure that their mortgage will be paid off at the end of its term.
ENDOWMENT	Monthly payments are just interest on the loan. Borrowers also pays a monthly premium to an insurance company for a life policy which should pay off the mortgage when it matures and provide a tax-free lump sum. There is a no guarantee that it will.	People who need more life cover and are prepared to accept the risk that the payout at the end of the policy will not cover the mortgage. Doubts have been cast recently on the suitability of endowment policies for mortgages.
PENSION	Monthly payments are just interest on the loan. The borrower also pays a monthly pension policy premium and undertakes to pay back the mortgage out of the lump sum released when the pension matures. As with endowments, there is no guarantee that it will.	People who are looking for a particularly tax-efficient way of paying back the loan – pension policy premiums are currently tax-deductable. But this will reduce the amount pension borrowers will have to live on.
INTEREST-ONLY	Monthly payments are just interest on the loan. The method of repayment is entirely up to the borrower, whether it be investments, inheritance, trading down to a smaller house or whatever.	People who have no need of additional life cover and want a straightforward, simple loan.
FIXED PAYMENT/ STABILISED	Not the same as a fixed rate loan. The rate that borrowers pay is different from the rate they are charged, and does not change. If the charge rate is higher than the payment rate, the difference is added to the loan, so that the total amount owed increases. If the charge rate is lower than the payment rate, the extra money goes to reduce the total amount owed. Over the life of a mortgage, the ups and downs should even out.	People who want to know exactly how much their monthly payment will be and whose home is worth a lot more than their mortgage. This is important because when charge rates are high, the total amount owed can increase very quickly. For peace of mind the amount owed should always be less than the property is worth.
DEFERRED/LOW START	For a specified period, payment rate is lower than the charge rate (see Fixed payment section) by a fixed amount, but will move up and down as the charge rate moves. The difference between the two is added to the loan, so that the total amount owed increases.	People who are short of funds at the moment, but are confident that their income will increase fast enough to cover the higher monthly payments due when their deferred period comes to an end. When rates are high, the total amount owed can increase very rapidly.

MORTGAGE RATE TYPES

RATE	DESCRIPTION	SUITABLE FOR
VARIABLE	Rate changes when interest rates in general change.	People who believe rates are going to fall, or who prefer to follow market fluctuations.
FIXED	Rate guaranteed not to change for a set period of time. Redemption fee usually charged if loan is redeemed early.	People who believe interest rates are going to rise, or who prefer to know exactly how much they will have to pay for a set period.
CAPPED	Rates guaranteed not to rise above a set level (the cap), but can fall below it if rates in general do. Redemption fee usually charged if loan is redeemed early.	People who want the certainty of a fixed rate combined with the possibility of reduced payments offered by a variable rate.
CAP AND COLLAR	Rate guaranteed not to rise above a set level (the cap), but can fall below it if rates in general do. Rate can only fall as far as a lower set level (the collar). Redemption fee usually charged if loan is redeemed early.	People who want the certainty of a fixed rate combined with some of the possibility of reduced payments offered by a variable rate.
LIBOR-LINKED	Rate linked to the London Inter-Bank Offered Rate, a money market rate used as the basis for a huge number of transactions. Usually changes every three months.	People who prefer their mortgage costs to follow market movements closely, and who understand that markets can be very volatile.
FOREIGN CURRENCY	Funds are borrowed in another country, at that country's interest rate, and converted into sterling. Monthly payments have to be made in the foreign currency, so they will depend on the foreign interest rate and the current exchange rate.	People who believe that interest rates abroad are going to be lower, and are prepared to take the risk that currency movements will not increase their monthly mortgage costs. Only for the very brave.

CHAPTER 4

THE VALUATION
AND SURVEY

THE VALUATION AND SURVEY

Key money-saving points

1 If you are having a Homebuyers' Survey and Valuation or a building survey telephone around for quotations. Fees do vary.

2 Speak to your lender and then negotiate on a combined survey. The cost of the mortgage report should be included or a nominal sum paid.

3 Pay for a valuation or survey only when you are in a position to go ahead with your purchase. Wasted survey fees can prove expensive.

4 Should defects be discovered which you were not aware of, or the property is valued at a lower figure, consider re-negotiating the purchase price. Your saving could be thousands of pounds.

5 A survey will give you an indication of likely repairs over the following years. You save money by avoiding a house with drawbacks that you are not aware of and which are costly to put right.

Why have a survey?

When you buy a house, the legal principle of 'caveat emp-tor' (let the buyer beware) applies. If something goes seriously wrong, you cannot ask the seller for your money back. To protect yourself, you need professional advice from a surveyor. This is doubly important if you are a cash buyer not having a mortgage.

If you are taking out a mort-gage, the institution lending you the money will insist on a mortgage valuation being undertaken on your new home. However, where a thorough and more detailed survey is involved, defects that could become a major problem in the future will be brought to your attention. Knowing about these at an early stage allows you to take avoiding action, as far as possible. Do bear in mind, though, that older properties will almost certainly have some defects and there will always be some degree of improvement and maintenance needed.

My advice would be to have a Homebuyers' Survey and Valuation on any house more than a few years old. Consider having a full building survey on larger properties over 50 years old and especially if they appear not to have been very well maintained.

When do you have the survey done?

Having surveys undertaken is not cheap. It is recommended that generally you do not consider paying your survey fee until you have a prospective buyer who is able to go ahead, (and his circumstances have been thoroughly checked by your estate agent) or you can otherwise proceed and buy straight away.

It will come as a surprise to learn that only around 15 per cent of the property-buying public choose to have a survey carried out. The rest opt to rely solely on the mortgage valuation report. Yet, while you might save money in terms of fees by following the majority, a survey can potentially save you much more.

Types of survey

When considering having a survey or valuation undertaken on the home of your choice, there are basically three options from which you can choose.

1
BANK/BUILDING SOCIETY VALUATION

This valuation involves the lending institution using a survey to check the property for mortgage purposes. Here, you will have to pay a fee based on a set scale dependent on the purchase price of the house you are buying.

Mortgage valuations are carried out in order to establish whether or not the house is adequate security against the loan. In a visit normally taking less than an hour, the surveyor will inspect the general condition and, with his knowledge of the local market and conditions, fix a realistic price on the property.

Any adverse factors that may affect the value and cause the building society or bank to withold part of the loan until rectified will be pointed out, but the sole aim of the report is to show that if the property were the subject of a forced sale on default of the borrower, the value of the mortgage could be realised.

As the loan is often no more than 90 per cent of the valuation and frequently rather less, it may not be of concern to the lending institution that major repairs may be required in say ten years' time.

It cannot be stressed too strongly that a mortgage valuation is not a detailed or building survey. As a buyer you should not therefore rely on this valuation as an indication that the house is free from defects or even necessarily worth the price being paid.

2
ROYAL INSTITUTION OF CHARTERED SURVEYORS/ HOME BUYERS' SURVEY AND VALUATION (HSV)

This is a 'middle ground' between the building society valuation and a full building survey. It was initially introduced to enable prospective purchasers to gain an expert's opinion of the pricing and condition of the property under review.

The report is produced on a standard form, amounting to several pages, where the condition of each major section of the property is checked and enables you as the purchaser to cross check your own opinion of the condition and value with that of the surveyor.

This report is partciularly useful during the course of negotiation for a house and may be instrumental in striking a better deal with the seller – directly or through their estate agent – if you draw attention to any faults revealed.

It may be wise if the report advises on certain defects to ask the surveyor for a more detailed examination of these particular parts since building work may be required. For instance, panels and floorboards might need to be removed.

Many building societies and banks offer the HSV scheme in conjunction with the mortgage valuation. Talk to your lender about the possibility of the two surveys being combined. It is quite possible to have the building society valuation included in the cost of the HSV report for a nominal charge (say £20) on top of the HSV report. It may well pay you to shop around on this point. Have the cost of the report confirmed in writing. Be sure to read the Conditions of Engagement carefully and satisfy yourself that these meet your needs.

Bear in mind that Homebuyers' Survey and Valuations have their limitations. While all parts of the property which are readily visible and accessible will be inspected, there will be no under-floor inspection (unless there is direct access); nor will an inaccessible roof be subjected to close scrutiny where its height exceeds three metres (10 feet) above ground level. Often, a HSV report will point to areas requiring further investigation (for example by a plumber or electrician to inspect the drainage or power supply) which could involve you in further expense.

3
BUILDING SURVEY

As the title suggests, this is a very comprehensive report and valuation on a house. A full building survey is an inspection and not a test, although certain items may well be tested. Sometimes building surveys are carried out by, say, qualified building surveyors who do not carry out a valuation. As part of your negotiation you may find it useful to have a valuation so seek clarification on this point. If any significant defects are brought to light they will tend to reduce the value and therefore the price

can often be re-negotiated on this basis.

The surveyor will often ask if specific items are required to be inspected in more detail, for instance, you might ask him to undertake electrical wiring tests, examine the drainage system, or check out the central heating.

The report is very extensive in content. For this reason the fee involved is greater than that levied for a HSV report.

There is no accepted standard presentation for a full building survey so you may wish to see a specimen report from the surveyor who will carry out the survey.

This report will be very detailed and reveal all the present and potential future defects you should be aware of.

Many building surveys are carried out on conditions of engagement similar to HSV reports. Read these carefully so you know exactly what you should be getting for your money.

What is the cost of a survey?

The cost of mortgage valuations, HSVs and building surveys vary. Most mortgage valuations are based on the purchase price of the property, but differ from lender to lender. Usually the fee is paid to your lender at the time of submitting your mortgage application and is passed on to the valuer and surveyor.

The HSV again, is based on the purchase price of a property, but this is also often adjusted by reference to the age of the property: the older the property the greater the fee.

The fee structure given is not normally rigid and can vary. The lender will be happy to deal with this issue, but be sure to negotiate directly if you are having both a HSV and mortgage valuation. Similarly, full building surveys are subject to variation and the cost can vary quite considerably meaning that shopping around could save you money.

It is, therefore, important if you are having another survey type carried out it is sorted out at this stage. Many lending institutions have a panel of selected surveyors who carry out their valuations. To save money on combining your report you need to have spoken to the surveyor *before* paying over your survey fee.

If you are in any doubt about what you are getting for your money ask to see a specimen report and talk the matter over with a surveyor.

When you have chosen your surveyor, ask him to confirm the instructions, the fee and the time scale for receiving the report in writing. The surveyor should, of course, be fully qualified (ARICS/FRICS) and highly experienced in carrying out the type of report you are requesting.

You can see, therefore, that surveys are not inexpensive. But see them in the wider context of alerting you to any major defects. Further, should a survey fail to expose fundamental faults then you may have legal redress for damages.

Don't let the table deceive you into thinking that there is a standard charge for building surveys. The opposite is true. A *Which?* report, 'How Surveys Measure Up', tells of a situation where firms were instructed to carry out a building survey on a detached four-bedroomed house. Firm 'A' took six hours to do the report and charged £431.25 (including VAT). Yet firms 'B' and 'C' each took half this time and charged much more – £569.25 and £557.75 respectively! Firm 'A' provided the best report.

In preparing the tables set out below showing the typical charges for the various surveys already discussed, I have collected information from a wide number of leading institutions and individual surveyors. This data will give you a good indication of likely fees.

It is interesting to point out that the fees are not necessarily increased regularly. Many fees are based on the purchase price of a property so as long as house prices tend to rise survey fees will automatically go up too.

TYPICAL BUILDING SURVEY REPORT CHARGES (£)

PURCHASE PRICE NOT EXCEEDING	AGE OF PROPERTY		
	PRE-1919	1919–1950	1950–on
40,000	320	295	270
50,000	345	320	295
60,000	370	345	320
70,000	395	370	345
80,000	420	395	370
90,000	445	420	395
100,000	470	445	420
125,000	495	470	445
150,000	520	495	470
175,000	545	520	495
200,000	570	545	520
250,000	620	595	570
300,000	670	620	595

TYPICAL HOMEBUYERS' SURVEY AND VALUATION FEES

AMOUNT	AGE OF PROPERTY		
	1875–1914	1915–1945	1945–1990
Up to £25,000	£140	£130	£120
£25,000 & over	£160	£140	£130
£35,000 & over	£180	£160	£140
£45,000 & over	£200	£180	£160
£65,000 & over	£220	£200	£180
£85,000 & over	£230	£220	£200
£100,000 to £140,000	£290	£260	£220
£140,000 to £160,000	£320	£290	£260

TYPICAL MORTGAGE VALUATION FEES

Up to £30,000	£65
£30,000 – £60,000	£75
£60,000 – £100,000	£120
£100,000 – £150,000	£140
Up to £200,000	£170

N.B. All figures exclude VAT

How do you use a survey to renegotiate the purchase price?

At the end of a report a surveyor will summarise his findings on the valuation. These will include any defects (if any) that he has uncovered along with the estimated costs of remedying these.

It is absolutely imperative that you are aware of the financial implications of setting right a flawed property. To do so you must read through the surveyor's report (and especially the conclusions) as soon as it becomes available.

These findings will provide your principal weapon in renegotiating the price. Make their source very clear to the selling agent if the sellers are using one or to them directly. Your case for a reduction in price will then be much stronger.

If a vendor refuses to reduce his price and defects mentioned are of a minor nature you may have to change your tack and buy anyway.

First-time buyers can be badly affected by low valuations if a seller will not come down in price. Banks and building societies lend only a proportion of the surveyor's valuation not the agreed selling price. For instance, a first-time buyer who agrees to buy a flat for £50,000 may need a mortgage of 90 per cent of the selling price. If the surveyor then values the flat at £45,000 he can borrow less than he thought. Instead of being offered a mortgage of £45,000 he can only raise £40,500.

You could always consider having another valuation undertaken, possibly using another lender and surveyor in such a situation, but this is going to be costly.

The legal position with surveys

In recent years there have been a number of well-publicised court cases regarding negligent surveys.

A valuer carrying out an inspection of a property for mortgage purposes owes a legal duty of care to the prospective buyer as well as to his client, the lender.

Although it is accepted that a mortgage valuation involves a brief inspection only of a property it should be carried out by a reasonably competent surveyor. The valuation will not be negligent unless unobserved defects that should have been spotted have a significant impact on value.

It would appear to be recognised that a valuation, while requiring reference to visible condition, is not regarded as being on the same level as a survey. This emphasises even more the need for you to have a survey undertaken.

Because of the legal implications of negligent surveys, surveyors often cover themselves by cataloguing every conceivable 'fault'. If you are faced with such a list, don't necessarily be put off. Separate the faults into the serious and not so serious. Some faults will have to be dealt with immediately, but others might safely be left for a while. The essential question to ask is: Will the cost of essential repairs be so high as to make it uneconomic to buy your proposed new home?

What happens if serious defects are found later?

If it is found that a surveyor has been negligent what damages can you, as a home buyer, expect to receive?

A home buyer is limited to a sum which reflects the difference between what he actually paid for the property and what the court decides he would have paid had he known of the defect at the time he bought it. The award of damages will not usually include the cost of carrying out the repairs in full.

The legal action over an allegedly negligent survey can be harrowing and costly. The Royal Institution of Chartered Surveyors have set up an arbitration scheme run by the Chartered Institute of Arbitrators. For a fairly modest sum (shared between you and your surveyor), the matter can be resolved. The arbitrator's award is legally binding on both parties and if you lose you cannot then attempt to seek redress in the courts. The scheme only applies in England and Wales.

Checklist on the condition of a house

You might want to save some money by carrying out your own inspection of the property you are considering acquiring. Should you decide to carry out your own survey on a house, make sure that you do this *before* submitting an offer. Always carry out an inspection in good daylight.

To assist you in this task, I have compiled a checklist to act as a guide. This should not be regarded as a subsitute for a proper survey. At the same time, by probing first yourself, you could save money in two ways. First, if major defects come to light you might decide not to proceed with a survey and withdraw from the sale.

Second, having discovered

various faults you could then call in a surveyor to confirm your findings. Look to use any fairly substantial faults as a bargaining counter to persuade the vendor to come down in price.

You will need a screwdriver for probing wooden parts – but be careful not to do any damage or you will be responsible for it. Binoculars are useful for inspecting roofs and chimney stacks, and spirit levels for the evenness of floors and other areas. A torch is required for examining roof spaces and, if you are able to hire one, a damp meter for checking walls for rising dampness. You might also need a ladder and steps (though it is possible that the owner might provide these).

Finally, you'll obviously want pen and paper to take note of your findings.

Plan your inspection beforehand. Basically, it is best to start with the exterior and garden before venturing inside.

If you are selling a house as well, have a practice run on your own property. It will help you in organising the sequence of your inspection and could alert you to possible problems when your present house is surveyed.

It is obviously necessary to carry your inspection out before a valuation or survey is undertaken. That way you can speak to your surveyor upon any matters which demand clarification before he looks at the property.

CHECKLIST ON CONDITION OF A HOUSE	
Examine front, back, left-hand and right-hand sides of the property.	
EXTERIOR **1** Chimney Stack Flashing to Chimney	COMMENTS
2 Exterior Roofs Flat Roofs (including Garage)	
3 Gutters and Downpipes	
4 Main Walls and Foundations	
5 Damp-proof Course	

6 External Joinery
  Facias
  Door frames
  Window frames	

EXTERIOR **7** External decorations	COMMENTS
8 Garage & Outbuildings	
9 Boundary Fences	

INTERIOR **1** Internal Walls Ceilings	COMMENTS
2 Fireplaces Chimney Breasts	
3 Floors	

4 Internal Joinery
   Doors
   Architraves
   Skirting boards	

5 Plasterwork	
6 Decorations	
7 Damp Condensation	
8 Woodworm Dry Rot	
9 Water, Plumbing Sanitary Fittings	
10 Electrical System	
11 Hot Water/Central Heating Age of Central Heating Boiler	

12 Roof Space
   Insulated?
   Evidence of Woodworm?	

Now let's look in more detail at each item on the checklist to give you a better idea of what to look for.

EXTERIOR

1 Chimney stack and flashings
Is the mortar pointing to the chimney in good condition and is the lead flashing at the base of the chimney where it meets the roof in good condition?

2 Roofs
All roof materials, be they clay tiles, concrete tiles, or slates, have a limited life. Where there are flat felt roofs these have a lifespan of not more than about 15 years (often less) and then serious damp problems can occur internally.

With any major roofing problem you discover, be sure to consult a roof specialist. If the roof deteriorates, serious damp problems can occur inside the property. If a slate roof is replaced with concrete tiles the original frame will need strengthening. Where this is not done, marked roof spread can occur.

Ensure that no tiles are missing or have slipped.

3 Gutters and downpipes
These are often of metal or PVC plastic. Leaking gutters or downpipes can lead to water penetrating the walls of a building. Look for clear gutters and downpipes and any signs of blockage.

4 Foundations and walls
Most serious problems in domestic buildings stem from defects in foundations with consequential cracking of walls.

There are two main types of foundations:
- Strip foundations consist of a concrete strip under the walls;
- Raft foundations consist of a reinforced concrete slab under the entire structure.

All foundations are affected by settlement to some degree. This can vary according to the soil type. If an old or ongoing coalmine runs underneath the property then there may be a danger of serious subsidence.

A large-sized crack (above one millimetre) or a large number of fine cracks can give cause for concern.

Underpinning foundations is a very costly matter. Be wary of trees close to domestic buildings especially in clay soils.

Walls should be well pointed to prevent damp penetration. Where this isn't the case then consider the extent to which repointing is necessary and, if you are not a DIY expert, ask a local builder to provide an estimate of the probable cost of putting this right.

5 Damp-proof course
The damp-proof course is installed to stop water rising upwards into the walls of a property. In many houses the DPC can be of slate, bitumen

felt or blue bricks.

The older the property the more susceptible it is to rising damp, quite simply because DPCs are comparatively recent and simply don't exist in houses dating back to before the early part of the twentieth century.

The most common treatment for rising damp is by silicone injection. A series of holes are drilled into the wall at DPC level (about 20cm above the ground) and a silicone resin is pumped into the wall. This then forms a solidified jelly impervious to water. After the DPC has been installed all plaster is normally stripped off the walls internally and replaced with a special waterproof plaster.

Rising damp is only found up to a level of a metre from ground level and can sometimes be seen by a 'tide mark' on internal walls. Sometimes there is no such evidence and the presence of damp can only be detected by the use of a damp meter.

If rising damp is a problem in a house you are considering buying there are a number of specialist firms willing to provide a free report on the extent of damp and the likely cost of removing it. Be sure to get several quotations and a guarantee on the standard of the work.

6 External joinery

Should woodwork be continually exposed to water wet rot may occur. Damaged wood

should be cut out and replaced with new wood and the source of dampness stopped or the woodwork protected by the use of sealants or repainting.

7 External decorations

If external decorations, especially woodwork, are not kept up to standard problems such as wet rot will be stimulated. External woodwork needs to be repainted every four years or so. Ask the owner about this point.

8 Garage and outbuildings

These should be kept in good condition. Many garages and outbuildings have flat roofs so be wary of these and inspect them closely.

Look on the roof for signs of splits in the roof covering, or for lifting corners and joints. Then look at the inside of the roof for damp patches or mildew on the joists.

9 Boundary fences/walls

Ensure that these are all in good condition.

INTERIOR

1 Internal walls and ceilings

Carefully check internal walls and ceilings for large cracks or obvious damp patches. If there are problems check to see if there is external evidence of faults. Plaster ceilings and partitions out of key often need attention.

2 Fireplaces and chimney breasts
Fireplaces obviously should be kept clear if they are in use. Damp penetration can occur around chimney breasts.

3 Floors
Most first floors in domestic buildings are of suspended timber construction. Ground floors can be suspended timber floors or of solid construction.

Solid concrete floors at ground level are often not part of the load-bearing structure.

Floors can move for a number of reasons including poor construction and subsidence. Major work can be expensive, not to say inconvenient.

Timber floors have clear voids below which must be kept well ventilated to prevent problems such as dry rot taking hold. Therefore, ensure no airbricks are blocked. If they are be suspicious.

4 Internal joinery
All internal joinery should be decorated and free from woodworm. Where rising damp is a problem, skirting boards can be affected by wet rot.

5 Plasterwork
Plasterwork is commonly damaged due to damp penetration, condensation, or by wear and tear. The remedy is to cut back the areas affected and replaster. This sort of work can often be adequately carried out by a DIY expert.

6 Decorations
If poor decoration is not the result of some other defect, then the actual structure of a building is not likely to be adversely affected. Any offer you put forward on such a property or the asking price should reflect the fact that the decorations leave a lot to be desired, and it will cost you money to replace them when you move in.

7 Damp and condensation
In addition to penetrating and rising damp, damp can occur in buildings due to burst or leaking pipes, or as a result of condensation.

Condensation is common in moist conditions where ventilation is poor. Condensation on walls is often accompanied by black or green mould. To cure the problem, the mould has to be killed off with a bleach solution and then warmth and ventilation increased.

8 Woodworm and dry rot
'Woodworm' is a misnomer because the 'worms' are not worms at all but mainly beetles and most types can fly. The eggs are laid in cracks in wood; when they hatch they turn into larvae, over time burrowing into the wood for food and shelter. The larvae then turn into pupae which become adult insects and find their way out of the wood, leaving a tell-tale hole. Eventually, over many years, the wood can lose its

strength as the holes accumulate and ultimately collapse because of the erosion caused by woodworm.

The most common form of woodworm attack is that caused by the common furniture beetle. This will attack both soft and hard wood so no type of wood is safe. On the other hand, the death watch beetle confines its attentions to hardwood such as oak and elm, which may be present in older prestigious buildings.

Providing the beetles' penetration has not gone too far, the harm they have done can be treated with an insecticide spray. Many specialist companies treat woodworm, but be sure to get several estimates for the remedial work.

Dry rot is a fungi that attacks and breaks down wood. It occurs in timber with a moisture content over 20 per cent and prefers damp still air where ventilation is poor such as sub-floor voids or cellars with no ventilation. In an advanced stage it smells musty and can look like a mass of cotton wool.

Dry rot often starts in inaccessible places and is only discovered when it is well advanced. Dry rot produces strands which can cross bricks and masonry. It is not localised in the same way as wet rot. With dry rot the wood becomes dry and crumbly.

A specialist should deal with the defect which will involve cutting out and burning all affected woodwork and treating timbers and masonry.

Contributing factors like poor ventilation will need to be remedied.

9 Water, plumbing and sanitary fittings

Water pressure should be tested. If it is poor a plumber may need to look at the system. It may be pipes have become fractured. All metals used in the plumbing system should be the same and not mixed.

Old water storage tanks may well need to be replaced though it could still be possible to continue with dated or damaged sanitary fittings.

10 Electrical system

The system should be checked after every five years or so. A qualified electrician or your electricity supplier should be able to carry out the inspection.

11 Hot water/central heating

Is there adequate provision for hot water? Central heating boilers may only have a life of about 12 years so ask the owner when the system was installed.

12 Roof space

Check the roof space for signs of daylight and weather penetration. Check that all timber supports look sound and the roof is properly insulated. Evidence of woodworm attack is something to look out for.

Case study 1

This case study is typical of numerous examples I could quote from my experience.

A property was for sale and a price of £95,000 was agreed subject to contract. It was an old house and needed considerable work doing to it.

The HSV reflected a valuation of £87,500 as being appropriate. However, it recommended that some £6,000 of work needed to be undertaken to bring the property up to a satisfactory standard. In this case when the housing market was fairly active, based on the HSV the buyer was able to agree a new price of £89,000.

Without the benefit of the report and valuation it was extremely unlikely that such a price could have been settled on. The cost of the report was £230 plus VAT but it was obviously money well spent.

Case study 2

HSV was carried out on a property which was on the market and the sale agreed at £250,000. A lot of work was required on the property and the HSV reflected a valuation of £220,000. The market was quite slow and the vendor was anxious to move quickly to a new property. A copy of the HSV was shown to the vendor and a new price of £225,000 was agreed – a saving of £25,000!

PART 2

SELLING YOUR HOME

CHAPTER 5

SELLING YOUR HOME: GENERAL CONSIDERATIONS

SELLING YOUR HOME: GENERAL CONSIDERATIONS

Key money-saving points

1 When considering the option of selling, getting the best price in the shortest possible time should be your main goal. You have more chance of achieving this if your house is exposed to the widest possible market.

2 When selling your house remember it is very important to focus your mind on the difference between how much you sell and buy for. If you can get a bigger reduction on the residence you are buying it **may** be worth selling yours for slightly less than you would have liked.

3 Try and sell in the first half of the year if at all possible.

4 Recognise your strengths and weaknesses and relate these to the climate in which you try to sell – a sellers' market or a buyers' market.

5 Remember there is no precise fixed price for a house. Do all you can to ensure that you maximise the amount you sell your home for.

6 Try to avoid having two homes. Sell your own first before buying another property.

7 Avoid possession if at all possible.

Save money selling your home

You can save money selling your home:

1 By negotiating on the estate agent's fees. Examples are given later. You could stand to save several hundred pounds;

2 By negotiating on legal fees. In many cases you will avoid spending considerable sums not by direct negotiating but simply by ringing around!

3 By selling your home *providing* you still get the maximum price possible;

4 By understanding the house market you are selling in and by being able to negotiate from a position of strength and not conceding anything unnecessarily;

5 By understanding that once your home is sold you are in the strongest position to save money in buying your next residence.

Make money selling houses

Among the most significant ways are:

1 By buying wisely in the first place;

2 By improving or renovating an older property and selling it at a profit;

3 Through presenting your home in the best possible way;

4 By judging the housing market and knowing the best time of year to sell and exposing your home to the widest market;

5 Through knowing how to negotiate with your prospective buyer to maximise your price.

How do you sell your home?

If you have had previous experience of selling a property you will already be clued in to this question to some extent – but obviously looking to avoid unnecessary costs this time around. Or you may not have gone through the selling process before. Either way this book will prove invaluable to you.

The main steps to follow when selling your home

1 Decide that you are going to sell;

2 Finish off any necessary work and sorting out to ensure your home is best presented to sell it;

3 Have several free valuations from estate agents;

4 Decide by what means and who is going to sell your home;

5 Notify your solicitor;

6 Place your home on the market;

7 Show prospective viewers around and negotiate a price;

8 Notify solicitors. At this stage if you are also buying a house you can firm up on any negotiations;

9 Plan the move;

10 Complete the transaction!

Reasons for selling your house

It is worth considering the reasons why you may want to sell your house. Broadly, these fall into two categories: urgent and non-urgent. If you have to move quickly, for whatever reason, then you will have to make the best of the market conditions available. On the other hand, as you will see later in the book, if you are able to time your entry into the property market then, potentially, you can make and save more money.

So, let's look first at the more pressing reasons why you feel compelled to move.

1 You have taken a new job outside the area. An estimated one in six people move for this reason;

2 Death, divorce or emigration. It is estimated that some 300,000 or so houses in the UK change hands for these reasons every year;

3 You can no longer afford your mortgage and have to seek either a smaller property to reduce your financial obligations, rented accommodation or live with family/friends until your circumstances improve.

Less essential reasons for selling your property will generally fall into the following categories.

1 Your present home is no longer large enough for your needs and you require somewhere bigger (and vice-versa). Clearly here a move is desirable as soon as possible but, unlike the preceding reasons, some flexibility over timing is still possible.

2 You realise that your house is the biggest investment you will ever make and the sooner you move upmarket the better. This reason is still given by most people for wanting to move. At the same time, you can still decide *when* to sell.

3 You wish to cash in on your investment. Here the property may not be your own, but has been inherited, perhaps through the death of close relations. In 1980 bricks and mortar made up £2.16 billion of the inheritances received in Britain. By 2000, it was estimated that this figure had leaped to £28 billion.

What people are looking for when they sell their home

Whatever the reasons for selling, you must have clearly defined goals that you want to achieve from a sale. There are four main ones and these will form the core themes of this part of the book. They are:

(a) the best possible price;

(b) a speedy rather than a protracted sale;

(c) the least hassle;

(d) the need to keep the cost of selling as low as possible.

You will need to be flexible and to match up different goals one against the other. For example, normally you will be buying another property at the same time as you are selling your existing residence. Let's say that the property you wish to purchase is available for some £5,000 less than the price you would be willing to pay.

Obviously you need to sell your property or the move may fall through. In this situation you can knock down the price of your home by several thousand pounds to encourage a sale. Here, if you slashed £5,000 off the price you would be no worse off.

The moral is that the most important consideration is the difference between the selling and buying prices.

The quickest possible sale may not be your goal if you are in no rush to sell. There are plenty of people in this position who take their properties off the market and wait for a better selling climate, or else have been frustrated in their search for a suitable new house.

What determines house prices?

Like all prices, house prices are determined by the law of supply and demand: the greater the demand the higher the price and vice versa.

A number of factors influence the price of houses. These include:

- size;
- location;
- plot size;
- condition; and
- tenure (freehold or leasehold) of a property.

The state of the property market in a given area, including the strength of the local economy, the national economy, or interest rates, can also have a crucial effect on prices.

Other important factors include how well an individual property is presented and seasonal price fluctuations.

Actual prices achieved in the market place (not asking prices which can be way over the true worth) are a good indication of what price is achievable. The more individual a property is, the more difficult it is to value accurately: its value is what somebody is prepared to pay.

To obtain the best possible price for a home means that it needs to be exposed to the widest possible market: the more people that see it, the better the chance of achieving a sale at the best price.

How to avoid possession of your home

The 1990s saw record numbers of UK homes taken into possession by mortgagees.

Analysts didn't have far to look for the cause. The tragic situation coincided with serious mortgage arrears, with record numbers of people falling between six months and a year behind in their scheduled payments.

Interest rates had been high for a long period, while a very depressed property market prevented many people from selling their homes and moving downmarket. In many cases, the fall in property prices was such that mortgages exceeded the current value of homes!

All of this followed on from the mid 1980s when conditions for a housing boom were perfect:

- falling interest rates;
- easy credit;
- large numbers of young couples entering the market; and
- a tax system favouring home ownership.

The message is clear: do not overstretch yourself financially when taking on a mortgage. Put down as much as you can. It's better to borrow 80 per cent of the value of a house than 90 per cent. That way, if you do get into difficulties, your lender is liable to be patient for longer, giving you more breathing space.

Possibly you will already have made this mistake. Other typical circumstances leading to mortgage repayment difficulties are:

- redundancy;
- a sudden and significant drop in earnings; and
- marital difficulties.

Whatever the reason for the problem, you should talk to your lender as soon as possible. The longer you leave it the worse the problem will become. For instance, after three months of non-payments some lenders impose an additional fee (around 2 per cent of the total outstanding). Don't indulge in wishful thinking and somehow believe matters will resolve themselves. They just won't. Even if you can't afford to pay the full monthly mortgage repayment, it's best to pay something. That at least demonstrates to your lender you are making an effort.

Bear in mind too that the lender will only wish to take possession as a last resort and will prefer to pursue other options first. The steps a lender can take to help will vary according to personal circumstances, the type of mortgage, and the cause of the payment problem.

Sometimes it is possible to peg payments at a lower interest rate for a period of time. A lender may even be prepared to suspend payments for a short period. Arrears balances can also be added to the main loan in certain circumstances.

If you have lost your job it may be possible to get assistance from the DSS. Government help with mortgages is available if you are on Income Support. Again, your lender may be able to point you in the right direction. Note, however, that no payments are made for endowment or pension policies connected with the loan. Should you or your partner have savings above a certain amount you cannot receive Income Support. Details are available at DSS offices.

It may be worth you taking on a temporary part-time job or considering accommodating lodgers to ease your plight.

If your circumstances are absolutely desperate, you could try letting your home out for a period and either move into rented accommodation, or stay with relatives or friends. Taking out an assured shorthold lease will ensure that the house becomes available to you when you require it.

In the case of an endowment mortgage, try to persuade the life assurance company to temporarily freeze endowment payment. Most will consider doing this for up to a year. If the endowment policy has been running for some time, it could be possible to cash it in for a respectable amount of money (though the amount will vary from company to company) and use this to reduce the size of the mortgage.

Voluntary and forced possession

Too many people aren't aware of the full implications of voluntary possession. On average around 40 per cent of possessions are voluntary. But, as often as not, handing in the house keys to a lender won't end the difficulties. First, if you fail to consult your lender, legal action could follow. Second, your lender is under no obligation to sell the property immediately and might decide to wait until the market picks up to its liking. Until the house is sold, you will still have to meet your mortgage payments. Third, it is possible that the house will be sold at auction for a much lower figure than you might have raised through a personal sale. Last, your local council, perhaps with a long housing waiting list, could deem that you have made yourself voluntarily homeless and feel no obligation to rehouse you.

To secure a forced possession, your lender has to obtain a Court Order. This will involve your case being heard in court. Here, your best move would be to seek advice from your local Citizens' Advice Bureau, who will have a free debt-counselling service and can direct you to special Money Advice Centres. As well as advising you, these can negotiate directly with your lender with a view to reaching an agreement. In such an event, the Order will be suspended. There could also be schemes whereby you sell your home to a housing association but remain living in it for a rent. At some future date, it might be possible to buy your home back.

If your case does come to court, be sure to attend in person should you be unable to afford a lawyer to act on your behalf. This won't guarantee that you'll win a reprieve, but it's your last chance. Failure to make a case at all will almost certainly lead the court to endorse the possession. Then you'll be obliged to leave your home by the date given in the Order. And, as with voluntary possessions, you'll remain tied to your mortgage until the house is sold. Moreover, in both types of possessions, if the property is sold for less than you owe, you'll be liable for the difference.

Should your house be possessed it may make it very difficult for you to get a mortgage in the future. Where an eviction results from a Court Order, the possession is recorded on a central register, operated by the Registry Trust, which is the source for the main credit reference agencies. Moreover, the Council of Mortgage Lenders has begun its own register of possessions to cover voluntary cases. If you have any complaints about possession then you can contact the Office of the Building Society Ombudsman (see addresses at the back of the book).

Sell before your home is possessed

Selling your house yourself and moving downmarket into a lower valued property, or perhaps into rented accommodation, is your best option if you don't see your financial position improving. That way you're likely to get a much better price than if you opt for voluntary possession or delay acting until compulsory possession is upon you.

Presentation is all important in achieving the best price and if you vacate your home then it can only deteriorate. There's a saying that 'nothing's as cold as an empty house'. It's not literally true, but the longer a dwelling stands empty, the harder it will become to sell it at a reasonable price. Dirty windows, cobwebbed walls, uncut grass, sprawling weeds –

these are all weapons a buyer will use to knock down the selling price. Worse still, your home might be vandalised, or uninvited guests could move in.

Lending institutions can take over a year to sell a possessed home and on average they only achieve about 70 per cent of the open market valuation. What you must do is to recognise your problems at an early stage and act (sell) before possession becomes your only option.

Finally, on the principle that 'prevention is better than cure', you could insure yourself against loss of income through being made redundant.

Redundancy packages and income protection plans are available. There are also specif-ic redundancy plans for home-owners. Some lending institutions also offer mortgage payment protection schemes. Remember, though, that you probably won't be able to claim on this type of insurance if you are made redundant soon after taking out a policy. Nor do they usually cover voluntary redundancy. The policies are useful as a temporary respite, though your mortgage repayments will be met for a limited period only.

If you find yourself in deep financial trouble take advice from your solicitor or seek the free counsel of the Citizens' Advice Bureau before parting with cash. Some of the organisations with the least legal claims pursue debtors in the hardest possible way!

How to deal with negative equity

THE PROBLEM

When a person's mortgage exceeds the market value of that person's house the term 'negative equity' is applied. It is estimated that by the start of 1993 the number of households in this unfortunate position was some 1.8 million By late 1996 with prices rising very slowly the estimated number of negative equity households was still over 1.3 million. The average amount of the negative equity debt was £7,000 although in London and the South East the figure was nearer £10,000. Many others are stuck because they are only just clear of the debt trap, as they do not have enough equity to cover moving costs.

Endowment mortgages are blamed for a large part of the negative equity problem. An endowment mortgage does not pay off any of the loan amount until the endowment policy matures, normally after 25 years. With a repayment mortgage, although most of the early payments are mainly interest payments at least some debt is being paid off. It is estimated that six years after starting a typical repayment mortgage, 10 per cent of the original debt will have been paid off.

So, if you find yourself in negative equity what can be done to deal with the problem? The first thing to remember is that if you are happy living where you are or can wait, there may be no real problem other than the psychological problem of living in a property whose value is less than the value of your mortgage.

Providing you can afford to make your regular repayments, over time the value of your home may increase. But what if you do need to move home for job or family reasons?

The one thing you must not do under any circumstances when dealing with a negative equity problem is hand the keys back to the lender, for the very same reasons discussed in the previous section on avoiding possession. Any negative equity dispute is a matter between a lender and a borrower but the borrower is obliged to pay back loans. If loans are not paid back this may be picked up by a credit reference agency. Lending institutions have up to 12 years to chase bad debts.

OPTION 1

Talk to your existing lender to see if they offer a scheme to allow you to move and take your negative equity with you.

In the vast majority of cases you will be tied in to your original lender but some institutions may consider granting a loan even if the original loan is not with them. You may have to be in a recognised profession for this option to be available. You should check that the interest rate you will be charged is the basic rate and not a higher rate.

It should be borne in mind that for any scheme to be considered you need to have maintained all of your mortgage repayments. If you have failed to do this you are likely to be refused any new loan.

OPTION 2

Borrow the money to eliminate the negative equity. If you are keen to move house one option is to borrow a sum of money to 'pay off' your negative equity. This depends on indivudal circumstances. A very obvious example would be to borrow the money from parents or close relatives. If you are of good financial standing an unsecured bank loan may be a possible option.

If you have other savings or assets it may be worth cashing them in to raise capital. You might, for example, sell a motor car and trade down to a cheaper vehicle.

Always check with your lender when the best time is to pay off any debt. Some lenders may only credit capital payments at the end of their year.

OPTION 3

Make larger payments to reduce the outstanding debt.

Many people suffering from negative equity took out their mortgages in the late 1980s and very early 1990s when interest rates were at their peak. If you can afford to pay at this level – or ideally increase it – then mortgage debt can be greatly reduced over a relatively short period of time.

OPTION 4

Sell your home using the advice offered in this book and look to rent. Many lenders will allow borrowers to take an outstanding debt and to repay it over several years. This option should, of course, be fully discussed with your lender beforehand.

OPTION 5

Swap an endowment or pension mortgage for a repayment mortgage. This advice goes against conventional wisdom that says such a move is a very last resort to be avoided if at all possible. However, if you need to move and the other options discussed are not suitable then desperate remedies require desperate measures.

Depending on the type and length of an endowment mortgage, it may be possible to sell it on the growing second-hand endowment market. An alternative option may be to make it paid up. This means no more premiums need be made but the maturity date will remain the same.

With a pension mortgage you might consider suspending the pension payments and restart them again at such time as you have eliminated the negative equity.

CHAPTER 6

PRESENTING AND MAINTAINING YOUR HOME

PRESENTING AND MAINTAINING YOUR HOME

Key money-saving points

1 Presentation of your home is crucial to selling it at the maximum possible price within the shortest possible time. Up to around 10 per cent of the price you achieve can depend on how well your home is presented.

2 Always take a look at new showhouses to give you ideas on the ideal way a home should look.

3 A spotless kitchen and bathroom are perhaps the two key rooms.

The importance of presentation

The presentation of a house for sale is crucial. Not only can it determine whether a sale is achieved, it can also make several thousand pounds difference to the final price.

My definition of presentation in this context would be how well a house looks both internally and externally, how attractive the garden is, how welcoming the house is (creating a warm and cosy feeling is paramount), the state of decorations and the standard of furnishings, including curtains and carpets.

Because in my experience up to 10 per cent of your price can be down to presentation, it

is important that we look at the subject in some depth. You only have to consider the great lengths to which builders go to generate sales for new houses. Showhouses cost many thousands of pounds to present and to staff yet their availability is deemed essential by many builders.

In a sense, you need to view your own home in the same light as a showhouse. Of course, it is unlikely that you will be able to afford to redecorate and refurnish to any great extent, but there are a lot of things you can do without involving too much trouble and expense.

First impressions are crucial

'You never get a second chance to make a first impression.' This saying may seem trite, but it is especially true when it comes to selling houses – first impressions are lasting impressions. I have spoken to many people who have said that within minutes of walking into a house they knew instinctively that it felt 'right' and from this feeling flowed a desire to buy. Equally, if the right atmosphere and presentation are missing, so a prospective buyer may rapidly conclude that your house is not suitable.

Basically, your house should be as clean, tidy and uncluttered as possible. Remember that you are trying to sell a lifestyle. If your house is in a chaotic state then you stand very little chance of selling it, unless your price reflects this chaos. But with the right preparation for a sale you can not only achieve a successful sale, but also stand to 'make' a considerable sum through a good selling price.

Externally

First, ensure that the garden is looking good. This won't be easy if you are looking for a winter sale, but in the summer months ensure that lawns are neatly mowed and meticulously bordered. A good spread of flowers, presenting an array of colours also helps to create the right impression. Expenditure on flowers and decorative plants won't necessarily cost the earth.

By the same token, don't be afraid to take out trees or shrubs which obscure views. What you are looking for is to create a feeling of space. Trees should be planted on the boundary of the property. Conifers are a particular favourite, but if you employ these do go for different shapes and colours to create a visually interesting effect. The same applies to shrubs.

Bear in mind, too, that gardens need maintaining. Not all your potential buyers are going to be keen gardeners and could well be put off by the thought of a lot of gardening work. Such buyers tend to prefer a simple garden where a lawn takes up most of the ground, with a slabbed path running up it to the house. Large lawns also contribute to the feeling of space. Try to keep flower beds to a reasonable size.

Next, ask yourself whether the exterior of your property is looking good? This means no peeling doors or window frames or dirty door steps. Ensure windows sparkle both outside and inside. Any moving slates, broken or missing tiles, cracked window panes and anything else which is in a less than satisfactory state should be remedied.

But think twice before going further than this. Major alterations won't necessarily make your house more saleable and could well have the opposite effect.

Too many sellers don't bother about garages – but be assured that buyers, most of whom will be car owners, will give them a good looking over. Unless your garage is a large one, or you own a small car, a good tip is to leave your vehicle outside the garage. This will make it appear bigger that it actually is. Ensure that any oil stains have been removed, remove all rubbish and make sure everything is tidy. Allow the buyer to try his car for size if he wishes.

Internally

When choosing a colour scheme try to keep to pale neutrals as these help to make a house look more spacious and are restful on the eye. To move away from neutral colours only risks offending the buyer who will be put off by the thought of having to redecorate to suit his tastes. Full redecoration is not called for, but do repair peeling wallpaper and damaged paintwork.

All small DIY jobs should be attended to by replacing broken door knobs, sash cords, etc. Ensure, though, that any work on DIY lines isn't botched – amateurish repair work will stand out a mile. All light bulbs and electrical appliances should be in full working order.

Spaciousness

Make your home as spacious as possible. For instance, you might spread clothes out in wardrobes, leaving one or two empty coat-hangers. Get rid of all unnecessary rubbish and clutter. Invest money in mirrors to make rooms look bigger. This applies especially to bathrooms and at the end of corridors.

Bathrooms and kitchens are crucial rooms and can help sell houses by themselves if presented correctly. A well-equipped and sparklingly clean kitchen will help to bring about a sale. So too will a homely and alluring bathroom. New or recently cleaned curtains in a bathroom help to bring about this effect. In both rooms place a few plants. Given the choice, add a shower unit to a bathroom rather than a jacuzzi which, though it will create a talking point, won't add value to your house or be as good a selling feature.

In winter ensure that your

home is warm and comfortable. Turn up the central heating to a reasonable level or, where applicable, ensure that a glowing fire has been lit some time before the visit takes place.

Do not forget the underrated sense of smell

Creating the right 'feeling' also means eliminating all smells which might be offensive. Be careful to get rid of such smells – stale tabacco in the atmosphere of rooms can be very offputting (keep all ashtrays empty), so too can be animal smells, or foods such as garlic. Take care not to cook before an appointment with a prospective buyer.

If possible, have a pot of filter coffee available. Have plenty of fresh flowers such as freesias around your home which give off a pleasant and natural odour. Also ensure that the house is well-aired.

For cloakrooms and bathrooms pot-pourri and scented soap are very effective. Small bottles of revitaliser can be purchased from most grocer's shops and supermarkets.

You can also buy a brass ring that fits over lamp bulbs and gives off a very alluring smell. The smell of polish and a soft cleansing agent in kitchens can be very effective.

Keep your home well maintained

We have seen the importance of presentation in selling houses at the maximum price in the shortest possible time. Closely connected to this is how well a house is maintained.

Prospective buyers are likely to try to negotiate lower prices for what they feel are items of disrepair, especially when a surveyor alerts them to the fact.

Remember that even if you are good at DIY and intend to do any work that may be necessary, it must invariably be done to professional standards. Otherwise, while you might save money on maintenance, the end result can only be to devalue your house, creating an opening for the buyer to seek to knock the price down.

There are several DIY books on the market that are good guides on particular aspects of home maintenance. Many can be found in DIY stores.

Accompanying the DIY boom, hire shops have sprung up all over the country. From these you can hire out all manner of DIY tools. The cost isn't cheap and you'll normally be charged either an hourly or a daily rate. Against this, the quality of the tools can save you much time and effort.

Let's talk specifics! The main items to bear in mind are as follows:

EXTERNAL DECORATION

Doors and windows need to look well maintained. They will be made of wood, metal or plastic, or a combination of these, problems will arise as a result of old age or where repainting is neglected. Whatever the material used for doors and windows, moisture will affect them from the outside and condensation from the inside.

Check the bottom halves of doors (including garage doors) to see that they are not affected by dampness.

Steel casement windows are susceptible to corrosion, especially if they date from the 1930s when steel did not benefit from a galvanised protective coating. Eventually corrosion will cause windows to crack and hinges and window catches to break. Aluminium and plastic frames, a modern development, don't have this problem.

Your house will probably require redecorating externally every four years or so because of exposure to the vagaries of the British climate.

You should seriously consider having the exterior of your house redecorated if necessary before putting it on the market.

Remember, eccentric colour schemes look garish and will put off all but the most eccentric buyer. Go for neutral shades (white is best) Keep to those colours that are in keeping with the surrounding properties and there is a good chance that you will recoup much of your costs.

ROOFS

If you have any missing tiles or slates on your roof they should be replaced as soon as possible. Not doing so will only invite damp to penetrate into the building (leading ultimately to problems with internal ceilings) while the wind will take off more tiles from the affected area.

Roofs are either pitched or flat. In the past pitched roofs were covered with slates, clay tiles, stone tiles, wooden shingles or thatch. Today the main practice is to cover pitched roofs with concrete tiles.

Be careful with flat roofs. Many flat roofs on houses are felted, as are garage roofs and may only have a life of around 15 years – often less. Failure to refelt at this point will compound the ensuing problems. Any indication of water penetrating a flat roof calls for urgent attention.

GUTTERS AND DOWNPIPES

Most gutters are made from either cast iron, zinc, asbestos cement or plastic. They will be connected to downpipes that could well be made of the same materials, though the common practice today is to renew these with the plastic variety, so it is quite normal for cast iron gutters to feed into plastic piping. Where you need to replace piping, go for the plastic type – they are much easier to fit and can be easily cut.

Whatever the material involved, a lack of maintenance can result in problems building up. For instance, failing to protect cast iron gutters through regular painting will bring on rust. Any blockages are full of potential problems – in winter when water freezes burst pipes will be the outcome.

Often the cause of blockages are either leaves or silt finding their way into the gutters and downpipes. Once there they must be removed.

Prevention is better than cure here. Adding wire or plastic balloons in the gutter outlets can save you a lot of hassle.

It is important to keep gutters and downpipes clear at all times. Ensure leaves and other debris are cleared out and that there are no leaks. Otherwise, problems can occur with water falling onto and penetrating brickwork.

EXTERNAL WALLS

A common task that often needs doing is the repointing of any perished mortar. If this is not done then water can easily penetrate the walls and cause dampness inside the building. If your house is rendered or pebble dashed make sure that these are in good condition. Where the rendering has cracked or bulged out, you will need to hack it off and replace it.

New brickwork can sometimes cause a problem when a white powder appears, causing surface discolouration (efflorescence). This will go away in time, but you will need to hose the wall down thoroughly for it to be seen to best advantage by potential buyers.

INTERNALLY

Keep on top of decoration (neutral colours, remember), repair items like light bulbs and leaking taps, dealing with them as soon as possible. Otherwise, internal maintenance problems will accumulate.

One of the finest investments you as a homeowner can make is a regular programme of maintenance. Prevention is better than cure. For example, it is much preferable to paint window sills regularly than replace rotten wood every five or six years. Bear in mind that no matter how many features are added to a house its value will fall if normal basic maintenance is not carried out.

THE METHODS AVAILABLE TO SELL YOUR HOME

CHAPTER 7

THE METHODS AVAILABLE TO SELL YOUR HOME

Estate agents: Key money-making and money-saving points

1 All estate agents are definitely not the same. Follow the guidelines on the estate agency checklist before choosing;

2 Try and negotiate on estate agency fees. At least shop around;

3 Do not sign any restrictive agreements. If in doubt let your solicitor see the estate agency agreement;

4 Always have a 'for sale' board erected if possible;

5 Ensure that your house is advertised every week or fortnight and a special feature is placed on your behalf at no cost. Secure a prominent place in your agent's office/window;

6 Keep your house on the market and continue to let people view it until all surveys and valuations are completed.

How do you sell your home?

This is a simple enough question to pose. There are however three possible answers.

1 The majority of people sell their property through an estate agent. Under this heading fall independent companies and those owned by large institutions (there were many takeovers in the property boom of the 1980s) such as building societies and insurance companies.

2 Property shops, that claim to offer similar facilities as an estate agent at a fraction of the cost, are another option.

Although many property shops were short-lived (for instance, the Woolworths chain), others are very well established in certain locations. They remain, therefore, a credible alternative and we will be looking into their advantages and disadvantages.

3 Finally, you can sell

privately, either to a friend or acquaintance. Alternatively, you may wish to pursue the option of selling your property to a wider audience. Provided that you know what you are doing, this holds the attraction of saving a lot of money. In practice, as we will see, self-selling may not be quite so easy. Should you choose to do so, then you will obviously need to go about selling in the right manner, so as to maximise your chances of a successful sale. Later on a number of very valuable tips will be given should you decide to go it alone.

Who do you choose to sell your home?

The question would be a lot harder to answer without the benefit of this book.

Preparation and planning is important in any walk of life; but when you are selling what is almost certainly your most vital asset, it is absolutely crucial. In other words, at this preliminary stage you must put a little bit of work and effort into the venture. In the longer term you are liable to be well rewarded for careful planning and a proper weighing of the options.

Because estate agents remain by far the most popular party through which to sell property, they will be dealt with first and in the most detail. All estate agents are not the same. Using the 'correct' individual and company can make a significant difference to the price you eventually obtain for your home. Paying £2,000 plus VAT to sell a £100,000 property may seem expensive; but if by choosing the wrong estate agent you end up with £95,000, it is cheap.

In my experience, good estate agents obtain far better prices than any of the other methods of sale. Added advantages they bring are convenience and security – they can arrange viewings of property and accompany propspective buyers where required. They will also be able to offer you good advice if things go wrong.

Whatever method you decide to sell by, look through the estate agency checklist (see below) and arrange to have at least two or three free valuations carried out. Before doing this you should study the property advertisements in your local newspapers. From these it may be evident which estate agents are selling the most and you might glean an idea of the types of property that they specialise in. Above all, the presentation of the houses (so crucial to a successful sale) should be a major influence in determining which estate agent you choose.

Your next step should be a tour of your area in search of 'For Sale' notices. That way, if you don't already know it, you'll find out just which estate agents are selling the most property. It could well be that the more successful offer the most competitive fees.

After this, indulge in some window shopping by viewing the property adverts in an estate agent's window. By now, you'll have a good 'feel' for the estate agent you prefer. At the same time, outside appearances can be deceptive. Actually go in to estate agents' offices and request some property details even if you are moving out of the area. How were you received? Were the staff keen and enthusiastic? Enthusiasm can help sell houses.

The estate agency checklist –
Things to consider when choosing an estate agent

Filling in the following checklist will help you to decide which estate agent you should use to sell your property.

	AGENT 1	AGENT 2	AGENT 3
1 Fees Quoted/ No Sale-No Charge			
2 Agreement Form			
3 The Offices			
(a) Well located			
(b) Smart efficient staff			
(c) Clear window display			
(d) Prompt 'phone response			
(e) Mailing list operated			
(f) Adverts well laid out			
(g) Professional image			
(h) Good property details			
4 Negotiating ability			
(a) Enthusiastic staff?			
(b) Will they look after your best interests?			
(c) Ongoing customer care is good			
5 The Valuation			
(a) Experience, reputation and impression of valuer			
(b) Professionalism and enthusiasm			

	AGENT 1	AGENT 2	AGENT 3
(c) Valuer gives house a thorough inspection including outside			
(d) Valuer has evidence to support his valuation and a very good knowledge of the area			

The amazing truth about 'No Sale–No Charge' from the agent's viewpoint

'No Sale–No Charge' offers big advantages to estate agents. It is easy to administer – no more laborious records to keep of how often a property is advertised, for instance. It is also a good marketing tool on a par with High Street shops who draw in customers with the promise of '0 per cent interest' on their goods.

The idea of paying nothing if you do not sell (or payment by results) is sound. It works this way. The agent allocates a sum for advertising. Let us suppose this is £500 a week for a page in a newspaper (it could of course be much higher or lower depending on the particular publication and its circulation). The main point is that no matter how long it takes to sell a particular property or how many homes are withdrawn in a period the agent still has a set budget set aside for advertising. The regular newspaper spot will likely continue as long as the agent stays on a 'no

sale–no charge' policy. What changes is the layout of the page and the prominence given to particular properties.

How can you influence the advertising process? Generally it is the agent who chooses how often a property is advertised. Arrange with the agent to whom you have given selling instructions, that he advertises your home at particular intervals – each week, every fortnight or some other arrangement you are happy with.

Another point well worth noting, is that in many cases the estate agent can decide on which properties he would like a special feature on. This is a very eye-catching advert that will attract maximum attention. Ask your agent to request such a feature from the newspaper shortly after your home first goes on the market.

If you do have to pay a fee plus advertising costs be sure to clear up what you will have to pay in advance. Specifically, ask the agent if the advertising rate is the net rate they themselves receive from the newspaper. Some estate agents make money by loading the actual costs to them of advertising and erecting the 'for sale' board.

Estate agency fees

A key point to remember is that all estate agents are not the same when it comes to their fees. But you should also consider that a good estate agent will obtain the maximum possible price for your property. This could amount to several thousand pounds; at the very least, it will net you hundreds of pounds more. As you read on, therefore, bear these two considerations in mind. At the end of the day, it is what you actually receive minus the estate agent's fee which is all important.

It may come as a surprise to learn that British estate agency fees are among the lowest in the world. Fees generally range between $1/2$ and $2^1/2$ per cent. Elsewhere fees are much higher. In the United States the average ranges between 5 and 8 per cent (and can be as much as 10 per cent). Spain charges at similar levels while in Australia, the government supports a 6 per cent fee.

Typical British estate agents' fees

SALE PRICE	FEE AT 1%	FEE AT 1¹/₂%	FEE AT 2%	FEE AT 2¹/₂%
£ 40,000	400	600	800	1,000
£ 70,000	700	1,050	1,400	1,750
£100,000	1,000	1,500	2,000	2,500
£150,000	1,500	2,250	3,000	3,750
£200,000	2,000	3,000	4,000	5,000

Add VAT to these figures to finalise costs. Remember, also, that the fee structure will vary from one part of the country to another. The South is dearest. Here you can expect to pay 2–2$^1/2$ per cent inclusive of advertising, boards, etc. on a 'no sale–no charge' basis. By contrast, if you are in the north, fees are likely to be lower at between 1–1$^1/2$ per cent plus all the advertisements. In many cases the two types of estate agency charges are likely to exist side-by-side.

How estate agents' fees vary

I carried out a survey of estate agents in areas throughout the United Kingdom, telephoning a number of offices to see what sort of fees they charged for selling a house at £80,000. It is quite clear that in many places you can save considerable sums of money purely by ringing around. If you wanted to negotiate further the time to do this is when the property has been valued, but this may be influenced, of course, by how saleable the estate agent judges your home to be.

It was interesting to note that in some cities such as Birmingham and its surrounding towns, there is a mix of estate agents; those that charge a fee plus all costs including photographs, etc.; some that charge a fee plus only advertising; and agents who charge an all inclusive fee and operate 'no sale–no charge'.

In some areas, especially the North, it may be that you cannot find an estate agent who operates 'no sale–no charge'. But you will find that there is still scope to negotiate on the fees.

TOWN/AREA	FEES QUOTED		
	AGENT A %	AGENT B %	AGENT C %
Bristol	2.5 (incl)	2.0 (incl)	1.5 (incl)
Southampton	2.5 (3% multiple agy)	1.75 (incl)	1.0 (excl)
Birmingham	1.0 (incl)	1.5 (excl)	2.25 (incl)
Edinburgh	1.5 (excl)	1.0 (excl)	0.75 (excl)
Liverpool	1.0 (incl)	1.5 (excl)	2.0 (incl)
Cardiff	1.0 (incl)	1.5 (incl)	2.0 (incl)
Belfast	1.5 (incl)	1.0 (excl)	0.75 (excl)

The agreement form

All estate agents must confirm their fees in writing making it quite clear the terms under which fees become payable.

It is wise to ask to see an agreement form prior to giving instructions. Request a copy at the time of visiting an estate agent's office, or once a valuation has been carried out.

Wherever possible, avoid long contracts and do be sure that you can give a few days' notice to terminate an agreement. Be wary, too, of the trap of having a clause in your agreement allowing the estate agent to earn a fee for a certain period of time after the agreement is terminated, regardless of who actually sells the house.

Finally, ask and agree in advance about what happens if you introduce the prospective purchaser yourself.

The offices

Before instructing an estate agent or property shop, undertake an inspection of the local estate agency offices. Ask for some property details and have a chat with the staff. As stated earlier, professionalism and enthusuiasm are the key ingredients to look for from the estate agency staff.

Having satisfied yourself on these points, what else should you look for? Many agents do not offer an efficient mailing list, but you want details of your home going to as many prospective purchasers as possible. On a regular basis, ask your agent for the names and addresses of people who have received details of your house.

Within this there should be a hot list. This consists of people who can proceed to move immediately. Normally, they will be contacted by telephone by the estate agent.

As part of this process of trying to achieve a quick sale the estate agent can, should you so desire, arrange to show people around your house whether you are there or not.

You will already have gathered that the right promotion is crucial to a sale. Always have a 'for sale' board located in a prominent and easily visible position if at all possible.

Many estate agents rotate the photographs in their windows. At the time of giving your instruction negotiate with the estate agent to ensure that your house will always be featured in a favourable position. Surprisingly, very few people made this request in my experience. When they did I always obliged.

Negotiating ability

Do you feel that the valuer and their staff are going to look after your best interests? Be aware of the rules of negotiation referred to elsewhere in this book.

The above quality will of course come into play once your house has been placed on the market and prospective buyers have looked around and agreed to buy. Your agent must check that the person wanting to go ahead is in a position to do so.

My own opinion is that once a sale has been agreed you do not accept any higher offers. 'Gazumping' (effectively a betrayal of the intending buyer) has rightly become a dirty word. Just imagine how you would feel if the vendor of the house you are buying cries off at the last minute unable to resist a higher bid.

Skilled negotiators are likely to get the price up for you. They are in a stronger position to do this in booming times, or where a prospective buyer is convinced that this is their ideal house, and they are determined to have it.

Although your estate agent is your ally, never disclose the lowest price you would accept to sell your property. This advice applies even more strongly in the case of people looking around – give no clues or indication to them.

Insist that your estate agent keeps you fully informed

It will of course, not be possible to judge how well you will be kept informed by your chosen estate agent at the outset. You could discuss how well an agent does in this respect if you have used that agent before, or if you know someone else who has.

It is important that you discuss with the estate agents exactly what kind of ongoing after-service you will receive following their valuation. Don't just accept their word – ask them to put their promises in writing.

You need to know from your estate agent what impressions the people who have viewed your home came away with. Specifically, the reasons they chose not to buy. Conversely, the party who looked over your property may be impressed enough to want to buy. In this case you need the estate agent's advice on the merits of any offers that come forward and whether a reduction in price is necessary.

Once you have found a buyer it is crucial that both your estate agent and solicitor keep you fully informed of happenings over the weeks until contacts are exchanged. The estate agent will, of course, have to comply with current legislation.

The valuation

Getting the valuation of your house correct is the key to successful selling. Pitch the price too low and you may sell quickly, but in the process you could lose thousands of pounds. Pitch it too high and it may take a long time to sell, become stale on the market and may mean a lower price has to be accepted in the end if a sale is to be successful.

Much will depend, too, on the reasons underlying your

sale. Ideally, you will be able to afford to sit tight until the right price is achieved. But you may have to move quickly (for instance to a new job elsewhere), in which case a bargain price might be essential.

What is required above all is that the price should be a realistic one. Always ask the valuer to justify the price arrived at. This should be seen within the context of similar properties in the area. Obviously, unless your home has particular features (such as an extension) the figures should be roughly equivalent. Otherwise, you will be lucky to achieve a sale with cheaper alternatives available, especially in a slow-moving market.

Always wait to see what figure the valuer comes up with. Don't disclose the price you think is correct, or what an alternative valuer has quoted.

If there is one agent you would prefer to use, but whose valuation is slightly less than that of another agent, never be afraid to telephone your preferred agent. Ask if they would be prepared to take your house on at the higher figure. You can always come down in price; you can't go up.

There is no such thing as a fixed price for a property. Most houses fall into price bands, plus or minus 10–15 per cent, around a mean figure.

As indicated earlier, just when you put your house on the market will be crucial to the level of profit you will realise on your property. The worst time that you can sell is during a period when house prices are falling because of poor demand.

Professionalism is vital to experience. A property qualification is a great asset although this does not necessarily make the individual a superb salesman. If the person valuing your home is a reasonably good salesman; satisfies the criteria on the checklist; and is qualified; then you have potentially the best of all worlds.

Which qualifications?

The qualifications to look out for are the letters FRICS or ARICS, Fellow or Associate of the Royal Institution of Chartered Surveyors. To gain these qualifications involves high levels of academic achievement and professional ethics.

The other main estate agency qualifications to look out for are ANAEA or FNAEA – Associate or Fellow of the National Association of Estate Agents. This qualification is only available to experienced estate agents.

The benefits of experienced valuers are considerable. Apart from their professional integrity, they will probably be able to answer questions on building construction, essential repairs, etc., with great authority and knowledge.

Above all else, the valuer has to be keen, thorough and undertake a detailed inspection of your home both inside and out.

Survey on how people found their home

On a regular basis I carried out a survey of all people (buyers and sellers of property) with whom my estate agency dealt with, to determine how they came to find the house they were buying. It was surprising how the results from different offices were similar. Below is a typical result taken across four offices.

MEANS OF FINDING PROPERTY	NO OF PEOPLE	EXPRESSED AS PERCENTAGE
From visiting the office	52	33
First saw the 'For Sale' board	58	37
Estate agency advert	20	13
Heard from friends	8	5
From the mailing list	8	5
Other	12	7
Total	158	100

It was estalished that 82 per cent of the people surveyed were moving a distance of under 10 miles with 18 per cent relocating further afield.

This survey was carried out in the Midlands region and centred on the densely populated Coventry – Nuneaton area. The results were fairly consistent compared to similar surveys undertaken over different periods.

What do the results mean to you? First, a 'for sale' board, whether you are selling yourself or through an estate agent, is essential. More than a third of the houses sold in the survey were as a result of someone first seeing the board.

Second, the survey demonstrates how many people actually visited the estate agency offices. A third of sales were initiated from this point.

If we combine this section with those dealing with advertisements and mailing lists, in statistical terms that is 33 per cent, plus 13 per cent, plus 5 per cent, which equals 51 per cent. This is a significant proportion of the whole and makes clear just how useful an estate agent can be in effecting a sale.

It is also interesting to note how many people move locally and not any great distance. Again, unless you have a property (such as a mansion) which will appeal to people outside your area, then a local estate agency should attract all your potential buyers through its activities.

Sole agency or multiple agency

Do you instruct one agent or several? The answer may partly depend on where you live – multiple agency is common in some parts of the country but not others.

Sole agency (instructing one agent only) tends to be cheaper and arguably creates the best professional relationship between a good agent and a vendor.

Normally (but read the agreement carefully), under sole agency you are not required to pay the commission if you sell the house yourself through, say, a personal contact.

A 'sole selling agreement' could mean that you cannot instruct another estate agent for some months; it may prevent you from selling privately even to a relative without incurring the estate agent's fee. Because a 'sole agency agreement' tends to be more restrictive, an agent must spell out clearly the meaning of the term.

The arguments put forward against sole agency are that an agent may have a relaxed attitude to a sale because he is not in competition with other estate agents, although if the sole agency is only for a short term (say four weeks) the agent will still probably have every incentive to work hard for a sale.

Multiple agency is where you instruct more than one agent and the whole commission is payable to whichever estate agent sells the house. The practice is most common in London and the South of England. Perhaps the main advantage of multiple agency is that competition among the estate agents in theory should increase the chances of a quick sale and a wider market being reached.

The drawbacks of a multiple agency include the fact that through your home appearing in a multiplicity of advertising pages it could give the impression that you may be desperate to sell. This erroneous impression could well attract potential buyers who are convinced that they can knock you down in price. Sometimes, too, confusion can arise as to just which estate agent has introduced a purchaser. In this respect ensure that you are only going to pay one estate agent!

My own opinion is that sole agency on a no sale–no charge basis given to the *right* agent will receive maximum attention and the best possibility of an early sale at the *least* cost.

Rules and laws for estate agents

THE ESTATE AGENTS (PROVISION OF INFORMATION) REGULATIONS 1991 AND THE ESTATE AGENTS (UNDESIRABLE PRACTICES) ORDER 1991

These far-reaching regulations came into force on 29 July 1991. From that date all estate agents were obliged to give prospective clients a copy of their proposed terms in writing before taking instructions. If an agent is seeking sole selling rights or a sole agency then the P.I. Regulations set out the wording for specific warning notices which must also be included.

The estate agent must also specify how his fee account will be structured. The commission and any expenses element has to be fully itemised including VAT. The subsequent invoice should match the itemised estimate.

An estate agent also has to make it clear at what stage the 'earning event' (entitlement to commission) becomes due. This normally occurs when the unconditional exchange of con-

tracts takes place. Should it say, be at the stage of introducing a 'ready, willing and able' buyer, then another statutory warning must be included.

It must also be made clear how much, if anything, a seller will be charged if he takes his house off the market.

An estate agent must also let the seller know if he is going to offer services to a prospective buyer, such as offering a selling facility or financial services. If the prospective buyer decides to take advantage of such services, the seller must be notified specifically and individually, although the legal obligation stops short of requiring the potential commission to be reported or disclosed. The obligation only runs until unconditional exchange of contracts. Thereafter the seller's position is settled and he cannot be further affected by the estate agent's actions.

The regulations also mention other 'connected persons', such as a remover, whom the estate agent may recommend for gain to a prospective buyer. This information must be given in advance to a seller who, theoretically, if so inclined, could withold instructions to sell.

The regulations go even further. The Estate Agents (Undesirable Practices) Order 1991 requires *all* offers to be confirmed promptly and in writing, ideally the same day the offer is received. Details of offers should be given impartially and estate agents must not discriminate against buyers refusing tie-in services, such as arranging mortgages through the agent, or give misleading information about prospective buyers.

The idea is to give the seller time to decide which offer to accept and prevent the agent guiding the client's judgement to the offer that will give the agent the greatest chance of additional remuneration.

It will be an undesirable practice for an estate agent to fail to disclose promptly and in writing, if the agent, or a close personal contact is interested in buying a property.

It will further be an undesirable practice for an estate agent to make a representation which is false with regard to matters such as room measurements, tenure of property, proximity to services, etc.

So what does all this mean to you? If you carefully read this section you will know what an estate agent is obliged to do in law. If for any reason the estate agent does not comply with the regulations referred to, then you as the seller, have no obligation to pay the agent's fees and expenses without leave of a court. Should such a situation arise, you would be best advised to consult your solicitor.

More importantly perhaps, by being aware just what professional estate agents should be doing, you can take some of the main points on board before instructing your chosen estate agent.

You might even ask your chosen agency to confirm in writing that their company is going to comply with all aspects of the Estate Agents (Provision of Information) Regulations 1991 and the Estate Agents (Undesirable Practices) Order 1991.

OEA

In 1990 the Ombudsman for Corporate Estate Agents Scheme was launched. The move provides further evidence of estate agents trying to raise their standards and improve their image. Most of the large estate agency groups are members and are bound by a Code of Practice. The terms specify that information given in sales particulars must not be misleading, there must be no compulsory tie-in of financial services, all offers must be confirmed in writing, etc.

This is, however, a voluntary code with no statutory backing. For complaints to be considered, consumers must first attempt to resolve the problem direct with the estate agent concerned. After this stage the Ombudsman can make substantial awards if he sees fit. Many claim an ombudsman scheme can only be successful if it has the full support of the industry it represents.

In 1997 the main professional bodies in estate agency – the RICS and NAEA agreed that all their members would abide by a Code of Practice for residential estate agents. The Code of Practice has nine areas and covers issues such as seeking or confirming instructions and also when agents may or may not charge commission.

On 1 January 1988, OCEA became the Ombudsman for Estate Agents (OEA) when the scheme was extended to include small independent estate agents.

THE PROPERTY MISDESCRIPTIONS ACT 1991

The Act makes it a criminal offence to provide, without taking reasonable steps to verify the information, a false or misleading description of a property to a material degree. The Act sets out to extend the 1968 Trades Description Act, to property.

The Act applies to residential and commercial estate agents, solicitors acting as estate agents, builders, developers and others engaged in the professional marketing of property. The PMA 1991, is enforced by local authority trading standards officers.

The main aim is to ensure that property is accurately described. In particular statements must be based on fact not opinion, they need to be supported by evidence when reasonably possible; they should not be open to easily different interpretation and disclaimers will generally not be effective.

The Act offers one defence only – that of 'due diligence'. In order for this to succeed, a defendant would have to prove 'reasonable steps' had been taken to verify the accuracy of the particulars. For example, it would be unwise for an estate agent to claim that a structural survey had been carried out on a house two years ago on the say so of a vendor. Sensible agents will seek written evidence.

What does all this mean to a house seller? It is important that a seller checks the details prepared on his property very carefully indeed. It is possible some agents will want a certificate from a seller to say that to the best of his belief and knowledge he has not given the estate agent false or questionable information.

Other methods of sale: Key money-making and money-saving points

1 Consider selling by auction only if your house has unusual features and will thereby attract plenty of bids. On the other hand, if your home is nothing out of the ordinary choose another method of sale.

2 Not all property shops are the same. Find out what you will be charged before agreeing to a sale by one of them.

3 Try and negotiate a fee reduction if you opt to sell through a property shop.

4 If you decide to sell yourself go over the following section carefully. Ensure your valuation is correct.

5 Have an estate agent in mind should your efforts at self-selling prove unsuccessful.

6 Be very careful you do not under sell when selling yourself. Remember, also, that a prospective buyer will know you are not incurring estate agency fees and may expect a reduction in price.

7 If you sell yourself, pay particular attention to professional presentation. It is absolutely crucial.

Other methods of sale

SELLING HOUSES BY AUCTION

The vast majority of houses are sold by private treaty. Such a method is generally cheaper than other methods (auction and tender).

Auction sales are often recommended where there is a legal requirement to satisfy beneficiaries, executors, etc. A sale by auction is proof that every effort was made to obtain the best price. It is usually important that an auction is recommended where one can expect to generate a lot of interest in a property. Hence in a buoyant housing market it may be ideal for a thatched country cottage or house with land, but not suitable for a terraced or estate house.

If successful an auction has a final result. On the fall of the hammer the successful bidder is under contract to purchase in accordance with the terms and conditions set out in the auction details. A 10 per cent deposit has to be paid and completion will occur on a specified date – normally around 20 days later.

Auction sales are usually subject to an undisclosed reserve price and the auctioneer will normally reserve the right to bid on behalf of the vendor.

The disadvantages of auction sales are such that you should consider them carefully before choosing this method of sale. As public sales are scheduled to take place on a set date, they can exclude some prospective purchasers who might otherwise have shown an interest. This applies especially to those people who need to sell their property to be able to buy and who do not want to resort to bridging finance.

Another group who will be put off by a public auction comprises those who have not been able to complete their surveys, legal inquiries and financial arrangements in time for the auction.

Another consideration is that auction sales and sale by tender are often more expensive than sale by private treaty as the legal documentation is more complex and all the additional selling costs are borne by the vendor.

When selling by auction you are likely to be responsible for the selling costs. Under this heading will fall such extra items as additional room hire. However, there may still be some scope for negotiating the fee you are likely to be charged. Also bear in mind that relatively few estate agency firms can offer a comprehensive auctioneering service and that most auctioneers are professionally qualified.

The range of choice available will depend on your particular area. Where there are several firms able to undertake sales by auction, judge them on the basis of the estate agency checklist. Additionally, you should consider what auctioneering experience the particular firm has, together with the comments and advice of its auctioneer.

TO SELL OR NOT TO SELL THROUGH A PROPERTY SHOP

There are variations on the types of property shops. For example:

• there are some that provide a virtually identical selling service to an estate agency, either charging similar commission levels or slightly less;

• others are solicitor property shops giving an estate agency/legal conveyancing service often employing experienced estate agents;

• still others may be classified as 'traditional' property shops, in that they claim to give an estate agency service at a fraction of the cost.

As far as the first two types of property shops are concerned, it is relatively easy to judge their performance by following the procedure outlined on the estate agency checklist. You will obviously need to find out how legal fees are charged by a solicitor property shop.

A large number of the 'traditional' property shops failed within a very short period of time, the most notable example being Woolworth's property shop; others have become very well established in certain areas. If you are considering selling your house through a property shop it is worth looking at the estate agency checklist to compare what sort of service you are likely to receive.

Property shops often charge a set fee for limited press advertising. For vendors who want their property advertised regularly, then the price may rise dramatically. So check this point.

For the set fee, a representative calls at the house, takes details, a photograph and erects a sales board. A newly registered property may appear for a period in the local press and might feature in an individual property shop's own bulletin. An individual vendor often decides the price. The property is displayed at the property 'shop' (which is often an area of a large store).

Now let's compare property shops with estate agents. It is absolutely crucial that professional advice is taken on all aspects of the sale of your house. The importance of the right qualifications have already been stressed.

Essentially, accurate valuation calls for great professional skill. Too high a valuation will protract and stall the sale, but in the process hundreds and probably thousands of pounds will have been lost that could have been yours.

Thus, a person using a property shop may possibly save a few hundred pounds in agents' fees, but could lose many times more than this by the property being undersold. Moreover, if you are going to undersell, you could do it yourself and save your fee!

Regular advertising with a property shop can take the cost up considerably – with no guarantee of sale. Indeed, estate agents probably have a greater incentive to promote properties for sale because until they are off their hands they won't be paid.

Consider also that many estate agents operate from shop fronts and are concentrated together. These provide a natural drawing point for anyone looking for property to buy. This observation also applies to those coming in from outside the area who may not know where to locate a property shop. In many cases, your property is unlikely to be even seen. Compared with a good estate agent, therefore, you are narrowing the range of buyers. Should you place your property with one of the larger estate agents, then it may attract an even wider audience through its chain of shops dotted around the area.

In my experience estate agents are much better equipped to deal with the complications that often arise and need resolving before a sale can be completed. Let us suppose that a property is down-valued by the lending institution, or a retention is placed on a mortgage advance because certain repairs are necessary (for instance, a new damp-proof course or re-wiring).

These factors can all cause a sale to 'go off', Here the skilful estate agent can often manoeuvre so that the sale is not lost.

And what if you are faced with the situation of having sold your house but not yet being in a position, for whatever reason, to acquire another property? Certain estate agents who have large management departments are in a position to offer both vendors and purchasers rented accommodation should this become necessary.

The major drawback with existing traditional property shops, is that many require an up-front payment that is not refundable. Indeed, you could well *lose* money rather than save it by taking this route.

Such 'property shops' have a contract to advertise the house, not to sell it. Hence they have little interest in quick sales. They need a large stock to attract people to browse and thus encourage more sellers to buy space. As in most respects, you get what you pay for. Consider placing your property with a local estate agent if the property shop's terms don't suit you.

SELLING YOUR HOUSE YOURSELF

Finally, we come to the method of sale that *could* save you a considerable sum of money. You could be deluding yourself. You might 'save' up to £2,000 in agent's fees, but end up selling your property for £5,000 less than you could have achieved through an estate agent. In such a case you *lose* money.

Saving estate agent's fees can also backfire on you. The prospective buyers, aware of this, could well insist on a substantial discount before agreeing to the sale. This will apply particularly in a slow-moving market, which will place you in a weaker position. If you are desperate to sell then you might have to agree.

The time you are most likely to achieve a good price is in a fast-moving property market. So, unless circumstances force you to sell at another time, you will gain most financially through waiting for demand to pick up.

Valuation
It is strongly recommended that you should have several free valuations from estate agents. These won't cost you

anything but will hopefully enable you to set a realistic price.

If an estate agent undertakes the valuation be prepared for him to advise you to let him manage the sale. Here you may say that you prefer to try to sell yourself, but will use his services in the event of failure.

The estate agent's visit can also serve another purpose. Before taking the plunge and opting for a self-sale route, ask yourself whether you are confident that you can provide as good a service as he does.

Be warned that you could fall flat on your face. During my career I have had occasion to visit houses which their owners had unsuccessfully tried to sell by themselves. Quite often, within a short space of time, my estate agency was able to arrange a successful sale.

> To try and sell your own house will cost money – possibly involving several hundred pounds and with no guarantee of a sale. If you do the job properly, you will need a board, photographs of your house, particulars typed out, and a sum of money for advertising.

As with selling anything, presentation is all important. This means that your own 'for sale' board, particulars, photographs and adverts have to be very well presented indeed.

And to achieve this you will have to spend money.

The board

A board is very important. Have this professionally made. By law the dimensions should not exceed 0.5 square metre. Only one for 'sale board' is allowed outside a property.

Property details

Property details of your home should be typed out. You can base your details on those given out by estate agents. Keep details simple and straightforward.

Although the Property Misdescriptions Act does not apply to individuals and private sales, it is as well to stick to its spirit and remain accurate. Superlatives are only likely to arouse suspicions.

Photographs

A photograph can be included on your property details and you may also wish to use a photograph in any property advertisement you make.

Advertising

Ideally you need to advertise your home in the same section of your local newspaper as that used by local estate agents and on the same day.

On the other hand, there is an equally valid argument in favour of advertising on a different day, say on a Friday or Saturday, when circulation also tends to be higher than normal.

Because there will be so few properties in the advertising section – indeed yours might even be the only example – your house is bound to stand out and be noticed more. To be sure of this, buy a larger than usual space. Even if this does cost you that little bit extra, your trouble could well pay dividends.

It is important to be clear about what your advertisment is going to cost you. Remember that you may well have to advertise several times before you are successful. Where more than one newspaper is published locally, I would suggest that you first establish their respective costs since these tend to vary. You can then draw up an advertising budget.

You cannot be certain at the outset how much your advertising will cost you. Obviously if you achieve a quick sale, your outgoings in this respect will be considerably less than if it takes some time to offload your home onto a buyer.

In the latter eventuality, be prepared to change your advertising strategy. You could switch from one publication to another, change the day on which the advert appears and switch the photograph.

Selling via the internet

Selling property via the net is still developing. Many estate agents now have their own web sites and it is likely that more and more buyers, especially those living some distance away from where they are buying, may first come to see properties of interest on the net.

For those wishing to sell their own property, certain sites are emerging but normally there is a fee to pay for the service. It is also necessary to have the correct valuation before advertising on the net.

CHAPTER 8

DEALING WITH OFFERS
AND NEGOTIATING

DEALING WITH OFFERS AND NEGOTIATING

Key money-saving points

1 Once you have sold your own house, solicitors are instructed and everything is fine with the chain, you are in the strongest position to negotiate on the property you want to buy.

2 Remember that in most cases your first buyer will give you the best deal.

3 Never disclose anything to a prospective buyer that shows you are desperate to sell.

4 Many fixtures and fittings are likely to be of much greater value to your prospective buyer than to you. It may be expensive for your buyer to recarpet immediately, especially if they are mortgaged to the hilt, so this can be a useful bargaining counter providing you don't overplay your hand.

5 To avoid problems when the surveyor calls for your buyer's building society/bank valuation, negotiate all fixtures and fittings separately to the house price.

Dealing with offers and negotiating

There are a number of situations that can arise in the process of selling your house, where you will need to negotiate. These are:

1 Fees and service you get from your estate agent.
2 Fees and service you will get from your solicitor.
3 Negotiating with your prospective buyer on price and terms. This is down to you if you are selling your own house; or where you are selling through an estate agent but are happy to negotiate direct with your propective purchaser. However, many estate agents will prefer to do the negotiating themselves.

Negotiations: general principles

Negotiation may be defined as 'discussing with a view to mutual settlement'. As a house seller the people you will negotiate with will want the opposite to what you want. The estate agent will be looking to obtain the best fee possible, where you will be looking to pay the lowest fee that is commensurate with the best selling service you can afford. Again, the solicitor will be looking to extract a sizeable fee in return for his services. Finally, a prospective buyer will want to acquire your home if at all possible at a lower figure than you ideally want.

You need to be firm yet flexible and ready to compromise. Meeting halfway is often the outcome of such discussions, but be prepared to back out where your objectives are totally thrown out of the window. It is important, though, to maintain a pleasant disposition when negotiating. That way, even if you don't resolve your differences immediately the other party will be willing to come back another day. Remember also to leave something for the other person. In other words, don't burn all your bridges at the first meeting, unless you have decided that the other party is intent on riding roughshod over your interests.

To negotiate well you must be aware of the strengths and weaknesses of your position. If you are negotiating with an estate agent you are likely to get better terms when the house market is moving quite well. This will ensure that the estate agent is anxious to replace the houses on his books as quickly as possible. On the other hand, if houses are not selling at all well and half of the homes in your street are for sale you will have a much weaker hand. In a bad market you may well have to be more flexible on your price than in a good selling market.

Try not to close any doors. For example, if a low offer comes in for your home, avoid the temptation to dismiss it out of hand. Often this is only the starting gambit on the part of the buyer, who wants to test out your position. Often the buyer will be prepared to offer an increased bid.

Do not make concessions all at once. If somebody offers £10,000 less than the price of your house you should not immediately accept the offer, no matter how desperate you might be to sell. Should you do so, the buyer may well conclude that your home could be obtained for even less and then come up with an even lower offer. As in life, we all like to struggle for our achievements.

Never reveal to a prospective buyer your anxiety to achieve a sale. This might be for financial reasons – say if you have taken out a bridging loan. If you do, this will invariably result in a lower offer for your home.

Generally speaking your first buyer will give you the best deal. Obviously this can only be confirmed with the benefit of hindsight. The person who is likely to offer the highest price for a house is the person most keen on buying it. This is an area where the professional judgement of an experienced estate agent can be crucial. It takes intuition to tell whether the first offer is fortuitous and good and should be accepted quickly and clearly. Or whether to turn it down and hope to do better.

THE IMPORTANCE OF CURTAINS AND CARPETS

In negotiations to buy houses reference is often made to fixtures and fittings, especially curtains and carpets. Fixtures like these, if they are acceptable to the purchaser, are of far greater value, because of the potential for saving money, keeping them rather than buying new.

Should you be selling such fixtures second hand rather than taking them with you to your new home, then the buyer is likely to give you a better price. Removing them should be avoided where possible – there could be problems in taking them out and alterations will be required if you are intending to reuse them.

By the same token, the buyer (unless a first time buyer is involved) is unlikely to want to bring along old fixtures and fittings at least not in their entirety. Provided, therefore, the purchaser likes your existing fixtures and fittings, you will be in a strong bargaining position to obtain the selling price you desire, while offering the buyer substantial savings through avoiding having to buy fixtures and fittings as new. Have this factor in the back of your mind.

What makes a good buyer?

When selling your house it is worth considering what type of buyers you may come across and which are the best type.

1
FIRST TIME BUYER

First time buyers with a mortgage arranged in principle are often excellent buyers. It is possible that they will be a couple getting married in the near future, a factor that will make them anxious to buy, always provided the terms are right and they like your home.

Try and ask for confirmation of their mortgage offer, or when their surveyor is likely to call to carry out the valuation on your house. Problems can arise with first time buyers especially when they are borrowing a large amount of the purchase price – say over 90 per cent. If your house is then down-valued by the building society then difficulties can arise. For this reason, always agree fixtures and fittings separately from the house price.

2
A BUYER WITH BRIDGING FINANCE

Such a buyer is often in an excellent position to proceed straight away. Most commonly the buyer's firm will be prepared to provide the finance. Again, ask to see a confirming letter where appropriate.

3
A BUYER WHO HAS ALREADY EXCHANGED CONTRACTS ON THE SALE OF HIS OWN HOUSE

Such a buyer has a definite sale and providing he can obtain a mortgage should be able to go ahead quickly.

4
A CASH BUYER

Be warned that many people claim to be cash buyers when they are nothing of the sort. A true cash buyer is somebody who can pay whatever your price is without a mortgage and is *not* dependent on selling his existing house.

5
THE BUYER WITH A HOUSE TO SELL

In such a situation you should always keep your house on the market until the buyer is in a position to go ahead. Otherwise he may not sell or decide in the end not to move after all. By all means, exchange names and addresses and keep the person advised, but under no circumstances commit yourself to sell. Try and establish how long the buyer's house has been on the market. If it has been on offer for some time then obviously there is a problem in attaining a sale and you should be even more cautious.

6
THE BUYER WHO SAYS HE HAS 'SOLD' HIS OWN HOUSE SUBJECT TO CONTRACT

This set of circumstances is very commonplace and so expect to face such a scenario. Here, you, or your estate agent, must check down the chain to ensure that a buyer fitting into the first four categories is clearly identified.

The longer the chain is, the greater chance there is of things going wrong.

The advantages of negotiating through and estate agent

Many people, whether buying or selling houses, are very reluctant to negotiate directly. This is perfectly understandable. A good estate agent is trained to negotiate and establish common ground. It is also important for you to have time and space between the making and conclusion of a deal, which an estate agent provides.

The estate agent will also be highly experienced in checking the 'chain' of your buyer to ensure they are in a position to go ahead. This involves establishing that all parties in a transaction have sold their houses to buyers who can go ahead. All parties must have a mortgage agreed in principle, if indeed they are having a mortgage. If you are selling yourself you will need to verify this information, but it could be more difficult.

The valuation and survey of your house

It is likely that whoever agrees to buy your house will have a valuation or survey carried out. Banks and building societies will insist on at least a basic inspection and valuation before agreeing to lend money on a residential property. Only an unwise cash buyer would go ahead and buy somewhere without first having a valuation and survey undertaken.

The type of survey carried out will fall into the categories we have mentioned in Chapter 4 on valuations and surveys.

Showing people around your home

The main point to make when showing people around your home is always to be very pleasant and friendly. People do buy people first and whatever else second.

Of course, somebody is not going to buy your home if it is not what they want, but there are many situations where a potential buyer would have bought a particular property if the seller has been more courteous and friendly.

Try not to breathe down people's necks whilst they are looking around. If they want you to show them round fine, but only one person should do the showing; crowding four people in a small room can make the room appear smaller than it actually is.

Ensure your home is as well presented as possible (see Chapter 6 on presentation) and remember that ideally children and pets should neither be seen nor heard as both can destroy the buying mood.

Try to answer all questions put to you as truthfully as you can. If a prospective buyer thinks you are being dishonest or deliberately misleading, the buyer will probably be put off.

After the prospective buyer has looked around be prepared to progress the sale. Avoid offering alcoholic drinks as you may be finalising a sale. Instead, suggest coffee or tea which won't break the buying mood.

Be well prepared. Have property details to hand, photographs of your home taken at different times of the year, details of heating costs, etc. Ensure that there are no obvious distractions such as loud music or a blaring television set.

If the viewer wishes to make an offer then your estate agent needs to get involved, if you are using one.

Be aware of the security aspect when showing people around. Most people viewing property are, of course, perfectly genuine but it pays to be cautious. Be sure to know something about prospective purchasers before showing them how the burglar alarm works or where the safe is! Ensure too that you and your estate agent have the name, address, telephone and car registration number of everyone who looks at your home.

If you are using an estate agent and you prefer accompanied viewings these should be made via the agent. If you are not at home at the time of viewing, or if you are selling a vacant home, then, for security reasons, do ensure that keys are kept secure at an estate agent's office and not given out to prospective buyers and others.

Tips on moving

Once you have sold your home and are to move out, the chances are you will be moving to another house, whether it is one you have bought, or rented accommodation. Essentially, two choices lie before you:

- to move yourself by either borrowing or hiring a van;
- hiring a firm of removers to remove your house contents for you.

Should you elect to move yourself then, unless you or a

friend happen to possess a large enough van, your expenses will involve the cost of van hire and petrol. Obviously, the further you have to move, the greater your expense will be. Depending on the extent and nature of your possessions, several trips will be involved.

Where both long distances and many journeys are called for, not to mention the hard work involved in loading and unloading the van, you ought to consider the alternative of hiring a removal firm.

If you decide to go to a firm of removers you may have several options, from them conpletely packing your belongings, to them just loading and delivering.

The key point is first to obtain several quotations on the price for moving. It is better if the firm send a representative to your home to 'assess' the job in hand.

A further useful tip is:

• should you be moving from a large town to a smaller one, then you should carefully consider the cost of hiring the removers in the latter, as they could well offer a cheaper service.

Also bear in mind the fact that certain times, such as at the end of the week, can be particularly busy ones for removal firms. It is best to avoid these.

It is important that you read the contract for the move very carefully. Be clear what the firm is stating it will do and what the procedure is if the removal men happen to damage any of your belongings while in course of removal.

Many firms insert clauses into their contracts limiting their liability for loss or damage to very small amounts indeed. Many contracts also contain an arbitration clause which means if a dispute arises you cannot take the firm to court.

Before moving check with your home contents insurer that you are covered.

Alternatively you may need to arrange some 'one off' cover to take care of your removal.

It pays to shop around. Costs vary greatly. In the 1990s a **Which?** report was revealing. Four removal firms were asked to quote for a move within London. The difference between the highest and the lowest tenders was as much as £156! From Edinburgh to Birmingham the difference was even greater – £532!

USEFUL SPECIMEN FORMS

You will find on the following pages, a selection of forms which you will need to complete during the home-moving process. Lengthy, official forms are notoriously troublesome to complete, and people often become confused and consequently make errors and fail to bring out all the relevant points. Take a while to look through the forms here and familiarise yourself with the jargon, so that when you come to complete the real forms you are accustomed to the style, layout and phraseology and can approach them with the benefit of experience.

SELLER'S PROPERTY INFORMATION FORM

Address of the Property: _____

_____

_____

IMPORTANT NOTE TO SELLERS

* Please complete this form carefully. It will be sent to the buyer's solicitor and may be seen by the buyer. If you are unsure how to answer any of the questions, ask your solicitor before doing so.

* For many of the questions you need only tick the correct answer. Where necessary, please give more detailed answers on a separate sheet of paper. Then send all the replies to your solicitor so that the information can be passed to the buyer's solicitor.

* The answers should be those of the person whose name is on the deeds. If there is more than one of you, you should prepare the answers together.

* It is very important that your answers are correct because the buyer will rely on them in deciding whether to go ahead. Incorrect information given to the buyer through your solicitor, or mentioned to the buyer in conversation between you, may mean that the buyer can claim compensation from you or even refuse to complete the purchase.

* It does not matter if you do not know the answer to any question so long as you say so.

* The buyer will be told by his solicitor that he takes the property as it is. If he wants more information about it, he should get it from his own advisers, not from you.

* If anything changes after you fill in this questionnaire but before the sale is completed, tell your solicitor immediately. This is as important as giving the right answers in the first place.

* Please pass to your solicitor immediately any notices you have received which affect the property. The same goes for notices which arrive at any time before completion.

* If you have a tenant, tell your solicitor immediately there is any change in the arrangements but do nothing without asking your solicitor first.

* You should let your solicitor have any letters, agreements or other documents which help answer the questions. If you know of any which you are not supplying with these anwers, please tell your solicitor about them.

* Please complete and return the separate Fixtures, Fittings and Contents Form. It is an important document which will form part of the contract between you and the buyer. Unless you mark clearly on it the items which you wish to remove, they will be included in the sale and you will not be able to take them with you when you move.

Prop 1/1

Part I – to be completed by the seller

1 Boundaries

"Boundaries" mean any fence, wall, hedge or ditch which marks the edge of your property.

1.1 Looking towards the house from the road, who either owns or accepts responsibility for the boundary:

Please tick the right answer

(a) on the left?

WE DO	NEXT DOOR	SHARED	NOT KNOWN

(b) on the right?

WE DO	NEXT DOOR	SHARED	NOT KNOWN

(c) at the back?

WE DO	NEXT DOOR	SHARED	NOT KNOWN

1.2 If you have answered "not known", which boundaries have you actually repaired or maintained?

(Please give details)

_____

_____

1.3 Do you know of any boundary being moved in the last 20 years?

(Please give details)

_____

_____

_____

2 Disputes

2.1 Do you know of any disputes about this or any neighbouring property?

NO	YES: (PLEASE GIVE DETAILS)

_____

_____

2.2 Have you received any complaints about anything you have, or have not, done as owners?

NO	YES: (PLEASE GIVE DETAILS)

_____

_____

Prop 1/2

2.3 Have you made any such complaints to any neighbour about what the neighbour has or has not done?

NO	YES: (PLEASE GIVE DETAILS)

3 | Notices

3.1 Have you either sent or received any letters or notices which affect your property or the neighbouring property in any way (for example, from or to neighbours, the council or a government department)?

NO	YES	COPY ENCLOSED	TO FOLLOW	LOST

3.2 Have you had any negotiations or discussions with any neighbour or any local or other authority which affect the property in any way?

NO	YES: (PLEASE GIVE DETAILS)

4 | Guarantees

4.1 Are there any guarantees or insurance policies of the following types:

(a) NHBC Foundation 15 or Newbuild?

NO	YES	COPIES ENCLOSED	WITH DEEDS	LOST

(b) Damp course?

NO	YES	COPIES ENCLOSED	WITH DEEDS	LOST

(c) Double glazing?

NO	YES	COPIES ENCLOSED	WITH DEEDS	LOST

(d) Electrical work?

NO	YES	COPIES ENCLOSED	WITH DEEDS	LOST

(e) Roofing?

NO	YES	COPIES ENCLOSED	WITH DEEDS	LOST

(f) Rot or infestation?

NO	YES	COPIES ENCLOSED	WITH DEEDS	LOST

(g) Central heating?

NO	YES	COPIES ENCLOSED	WITH DEEDS	LOST

(h) Anything similar? (e.g. cavity wall insulation)

NO	YES	COPIES ENCLOSED	WITH DEEDS	LOST

(i) Do you have written details or the work done to obtain any of these guarantees?

NO	YES	COPIES ENCLOSED	WITH DEEDS	LOST

Prop 1/3

Please tick the right answer

4.2 Have you made or considered making claims under any of these?

NO	YES: (PLEASE GIVE DETAILS)

---

5   Services

(This section applies to gas, electrical and water supplies, sewerage disposal and telephone cables.)

5.1 Please tick which services are connected to the property.

GAS	ELEC.	WATER	DRAINS	TEL.	CABLE T.V.

5.2 Do any drains, pipes or wires for these cross any neighbour's property?

NOT KNOWN	YES: (PLEASE GIVE DETAILS)

5.3 Do any drains, pipes or wires leading to any neighbour's property cross your property?

NOT KNOWN	YES: (PLEASE GIVE DETAILS)

5.4 Are you aware of any agreement which is not with the deeds about any of these services?

NOT KNOWN	YES: (PLEASE GIVE DETAILS)

---

6   Sharing with the neighbours

6.1 Are you aware of any responsibility to contribute to the cost of anything used jointly, such as the repair of a shared drive, boundary or drain?

YES: (PLEASE GIVE DETAILS)	NO

Prop 1/4

6.2 Do you contribute to the cost of repair of anything used by the neighbourhood, such as the maintenance of a private road?

YES	NO

6.3 If so, who is responsible for organising the work and collecting the contributions?

6.4 Please give details of all such sums paid or owing, and explain if they are paid on a regular basis or only as and when work is required.

6.5 Do you need to go next door if you have to repair or decorate your building or maintain any of the boundaries?

YES	NO

6.6 If "Yes", have you always been able to do so without objection by the neighbours?

YES	NO: please give details of any objection under the answer to question 2 (disputes)

6.7 Do any of your neighbours need to come onto your land to repair or decorate their building or maintain the boundaries?

YES	NO

6.8 If so, have you ever objected?

NO	YES: please give details of any objection under the answer to question 2 (disputes)

7 | Arrangements and rights

Are there any other formal or informal arrangements which give someone else rights over your property?

NO	YES: (PLEASE GIVE DETAILS)

8 | Occupiers

8.1 Does anyone other than you live in the property?
If "No" go to question 9.1.
If "Yes" please give their full names and (if under 18) their ages

YES	NO

Prop 1/5

Please tick the right answer

8.2(a)(i) Do any of them have any right to stay on the property with your permission?

(These rights may have arisen without you realising, e.g. if they have paid towards the cost of buying the house, paid for improvements or helped you make your mortgage payments)

NO:	YES: (PLEASE GIVE DETAILS)

8.2(a)(ii) Are any of them tenants or lodgers?

NO	YES: (PLEASE GIVE DETAILS AND A COPY OF ANY TENANCY AGREEMENT)

8.2(b) Have they all agreed to sign the contract for sale agreeing to leave with you (or earlier)?

NO	YES: (PLEASE GIVE DETAILS)

9 | Restrictions

If you have changed the use of the property of carried out any building work on it, please read the note below and answer these questions. If you have not, please go on to Question 10.

Note The title deeds of some properties include clauses which are called "restrictive covenants". For example, these may forbid the owner of the house to carry out any building work or to use it for the purpose of a business – unless someone else (often the builder of the house) gives his consent.

9.1(a) Do you know of any "restrictive covenant" which applies to your house or land?

NO	YES

(b) If "Yes", did you ask for consent for the work or change of use?

NO	YES: (PLEASE GIVE DETAILS AND A COPY OF ANY CONSENT)

9.2 If consent was needed but not obtained, please explain why not.

Prop 1/6

9.3 If the reply to 9.1(a) is "Yes", please give the name
and address of the person from whom consent has to
be obtained.

10   Planning

Please tick the right answer

10.1 Is the property used only as a private home?

YES	NO: (PLEASE GIVE DETAILS)

10.2(a) Is the property a listed building or in a
conservation area?

YES	NO	NOT KNOWN

   (b) If "Yes", what work has been carried out since
it was listed or the area became a conservation area?

10.3(a) Has there been any building work on the
property in the last four years?

NO	YES: (PLEASE GIVE DETAILS)

   (b) If "Yes", was planning permission, building
regulation approval or listed building consent obtained?

NO	NOT REQUIRED	YES:	COPIES ENCLOSED	TO FOLLOW	LOST

10.4 Have you applied for planning permission,
building regulation approval or listed building consent
at any time?

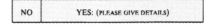

NO	YES:	COPIES ENCLOSED	TO FOLLOW	LOST

10.5 If "Yes", has any of the work been carried
out?

NO	YES: (PLEASE GIVE DETAILS)

10.6(a) Has there been any change of use of the
property in the last ten years? (e.g dividing into flats,
combining flats or using part for business use)?

NO	YES: (PLEASE GIVE DETAILS)

   (b) If "Yes", was planning permission obtained?

NO	NOT REQUIRED	YES:	COPIES ENCLOSED	TO FOLLOW	LOST

Prop 1/7

11 | Fixtures

Please tick the right answer

11.1 If you have sold through an estate agent, are all items listed in its particulars included in the sale?

YES	NO

If "No" you should instruct the estate agent to write to everyone concerned correcting this error.

11.2 Do you own outright everything included in the sale?

YES	NO: (PLEASE GIVE DETAILS)

(*You must give details of anything which may not be yours to sell, for example, anything rented or on H.P.*)

12 | Expenses

Have you ever had to pay for the use of the property?

NO	YES: (PLEASE GIVE DETAILS)

(*Ignore rates, water rates, community charge and gas, electricity and phone bills. Disclose anything else: examples are the clearance of cess pool or septic tank, drainage rate, rent charge.*)

13 | General

Is there any other information which you think the buyer may have a right to know?

NO	YES: (PLEASE GIVE DETAILS)

Signature(s) . . . .

. . . .

Date . . . .

THE LAW SOCIETY

This form is part of The Law Society's TransAction scheme. © The Law Society 1994
The Law Society is the professional body for solicitors in England and Wales
March 1994

Prop 1/8

SELLER'S LEASEHOLD INFORMATION FORM

Address of the Property:

If you live in leasehold property, please answer the following questions. Some people live in blocks of flats, others in large houses converted into flats and others in single leasehold houses. These questions cover all types of leasehold property, but some of them may not apply to your property. In that case please answer them N/A.

The instructions set out at the front of the Seller's Property Information Form apply to this form as well. Please read them again before giving your answers to these questions.

If you are unsure how to answer any of the questions, ask your solicitor.

Part I – to be completed by the seller

1 Management Company

1.1 If there is a management company which is run by the tenants please supply any of the following documents which are in your possession:

Please mark the appropriate box

(a) Memorandum and articles of association of the company.

ENCLOSED	TO FOLLOW	LOST	N/A

(b) Your share or membership certificate.

ENCLOSED	TO FOLLOW	LOST	N/A

(c) The management accounts for the last 3 years.

ENCLOSED	TO FOLLOW	LOST	N/A

(d) Copy of any regulations made by either the landlord or the company additional to the rules contained in the lease.

ENCLOSED	TO FOLLOW	LOST	N/A

(e) The names and addresses of the secretary and treasurer of the company.

Prop 4/1

2   The Landlord

2.1 What is the name and address of your landlord?

2.2 If the landlord employs an agent to collect the rent. what is the name and address of that agent?

2.3 Do you have the landlord's receipt for the last rent payment?

| YES | (Please tick box and send it with these answers) |

NO: (Explain why not)

2.4 Do you pay a share of the maintenance costs of the building?

| YES | (Please tick box and send the receipt. or demand. for the last payment with these answers) |

NO: (Explain why not)

3   Maintenance Charges

3.1 Do you know of any unusual expense likely to show in the maintenance charge accounts in the next year or two?

If "Yes", please give details.

Please mark the appropriate box

YES	NO

3.2 How much have you paid for maintenance charges in each of the last 3 years?

3.3 Do you have the receipts for these?

NO	YES	ENCLOSED	TO FOLLOW	LOST

Prop 4/2

3.4 Do you know of any problems in the last 3 years between flat owners and the landlord or maintenance company about maintenance charges, or the method of management?

Please mark the appropriate box

YES	NO

If "Yes", please give details.

3.5 Have you challenged the maintenance charge or any expense in the last 3 years?

YES	NO

If "Yes", please give details.

3.6 Do you know if the landlord has had any problems in collecting the maintenance charges from other flat owners?

YES	NO

If "Yes", please give details.

4 Notices

A landlord may serve a notice on a printed form or in the form of a letter and your buyer will wish to know if anything of this sort has been received.

4.1 Have you had a notice from the landlord that he wants to sell his interest in the building?

NO	YES	COPY ENCLOSED	TO FOLLOW	LOST

4.2 Have you had any other notice or letter about the building, its use, its condition or its repair and maintenance?

NO	YES	COPY ENCLOSED	TO FOLLOW	LOST

5 Consents

Are you aware of any charges in the terms of the lease or of the landlord giving any consents under the lease? (This may be in a deed, a letter or even verbal) If not in writing, please supply details.

NO	NOT KNOWN	YES:	COPIES ENCLOSED	TO FOLLOW	LOST

6 Complaints

6.1 Have you received any complaints from the landlord, any landlord above him, management company or any other tenant about anything you have or have not done?

YES	NO

If "Yes", please give details.

Prop 4/3

142

Please mark the appropriate box

6.2 Have you had cause for complaint to any of them?

YES	NO

If "Yes", please give details.

_____

_____

_____

6.3 Have you complained to anyone else about the conduct of any other occupier?

YES	NO

If "Yes", please give details.

_____

_____

_____

7 | Insurance

7.1 Do you have to arrange the insurance on the building?

YES	NO

If "No", go to Question 7.4

7.2 If "Yes", do you have a copy of the insurance policy?

COPY ENCLOSED	TO FOLLOW	LOST

7.3 Do you have a copy of the receipt for the last payment of the premium?

COPY ENCLOSED	TO FOLLOW	LOST

7.4 Do you have a copy of the insurance policy arranged by the landlord or the management company and a copy of the schedule for the current year?

NO	YES	COPIES ENCLOSED	TO FOLLOW	LOST

8 | Decoration

8.1 If outside decoration is your responsibility, when was it last done?

IN THE YEAR 19	NOT KNOWN

Prop 4/4

9 | Alterations

Please mark the appropriate box

9.1 Are you aware of any alterations having been made to your property since the lease was orginally granted?

YES	NO	NOT KNOWN

If "Yes", please supply details.

9.2 If "Yes", was landlord's consent obtained?

NO	NOT KNOWN	NOT REQUIRED	YES:	COPIES ENCLOSED	TO FOLLOW	LOST

10 | Occupation

10.1 Are you now occupying the property as your sole or main home?

YES	NO

10.2 Have you occupied the property as your sole or main home (apart from usual holidays and business trips) –

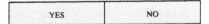

(a) continuously throughout the last twelve months?

YES	NO

(b) continuously throughout the last three years?

YES	NO

(c) for periods totalling at least three years during the last ten years?

YES	NO

11 | Enfranchisement

11.1 Have you served on your immediate or superior landlord a formal notice under the enfranchisment legislation stating your desire to buy the freehold or be granted an extended lease?

NO	YES	COPY ENCLOSED	COPY TO FOLLOW	COPY LOST

If so, please supply a copy.

Prop 4/5

11.2 If the property is a flat in a block, have you served on the immediate or any superior landlord any formal notices under the enfranchisement legislation relating to the possible collective purchase of the freehold of the block or part of it?
If so, please supply a copy.

Please mark the appropriate box

NO	YES	COPY ENCLOSED	COPY TO FOLLOW	COPY LOST

11.3 Has any letter or notice been served upon you in response?

NO	YES	COPY ENCLOSED	COPY TO FOLLOW	COPY LOST

Signature(s): ....

....

Date: ....

THE LAW SOCIETY

This form is part of The Law Society's TransAction scheme © The Law Society 1994.
The Law Society is the professional body for solicitors in England and Wales.
May 1994

Prop 4/6

FIXTURES FITTINGS AND CONTENTS (2ND EDITION)

Address of the Property: _____

1. Place a tick in one of these three columns against every item.

2. The second column ("excluded from the sale") is for items on the list which you are proposing to take with you when you move. If you are prepared to sell any of these to the buyer, please write the price you wish to be paid beside the name of the item and the buyer can then decide whether or not to accept your offer to sell.

	INCLUDED IN THE SALE	EXCLUDED FROM THE SALE	NONE AT THE PROPERTY
TV Aerial/Satellite Dish			
Radio Aerial			
Immersion Heater			
Hot Water Cylinder Jacket			
Roof Insulation			
Wall Heaters			
Night Storage Heater			
Gas/Electric Fires			
Light Fittings:			
Ceiling Lights	☐	☐	☐
Wall Lights	☐	☐	☐
Lamp Shades	☐	☐	☐
N.B. If these are to be removed, it is assumed that they will be replaced by ceiling rose and socket, flex, bulb holder and bulb.			
Switches			
Electric Points			
Dimmer Switches			

This form comprises 6 pages. Please ensure you complete all sections on all pages.   Please turn over to next page.   PROP6/1

146

	INCLUDED IN THE SALE	EXCLUDED FROM THE SALE	NONE AT THE PROPERTY
Fluorescent Lighting			
Outside Lights			
Telephone Receivers:			
British Telecom	☐	☐	☐
Own	☐	☐	☐
Burglar Alarm System			
Complete Central Heating System			
Extractor Fans			
Doorbell/Chimes			
Door Knocker			
Door Furniture:			
Internal	☐	☐	☐
External	☐	☐	☐
Double Glazing			
Window Fitments			
Shutters/Grills			
Curtain Rails			
Curtain Poles			
Pelmets			
Venetian Blinds			
Roller Blinds			
Curtains (Including Net Curtains):			
Lounge	☐	☐	☐
Dining Room	☐	☐	☐

	INCLUDED IN THE SALE	EXCLUDED FROM THE SALE	NONE AT THE PROPERTY
Kitchen	☐	☐	☐
Bathroom	☐	☐	☐
Bedroom 1	☐	☐	☐
Bedroom 2	☐	☐	☐
Bedroom 3	☐	☐	☐
Bedroom 4	☐	☐	☐
Other Rooms (state which)			
1	☐	☐	☐
2	☐	☐	☐
3	☐	☐	☐
Carpets and other Floor Covering:			
Lounge	☐	☐	☐
Dining Room	☐	☐	☐
Kitchen	☐	☐	☐
Hall, Stairs and Landing	☐	☐	☐
Bathroom	☐	☐	☐
Bedroom 1	☐	☐	☐
Bedroom 2	☐	☐	☐
Bedroom 3	☐	☐	☐
Bedroom 4			
Other Rooms (state which)			
1	☐	☐	☐

SPECIMEN

	INCLUDED IN THE SALE	EXCLUDED FROM THE SALE	NONE AT THE PROPERTY
2	☐	☐	☐
3	☐	☐	☐
Storage Units in Kitchen			
Kitchen Fitments:			
Fitted Cupboards and Shelves	☐	☐	☐
Refrigerator/ Fridge-Freezer	☐	☐	☐
Oven	☐	☐	☐
Extractor Hood	☐	☐	☐
Hob	☐	☐	☐
Cutlery Rack	☐	☐	☐
Spice Rack	☐	☐	☐
Other (state which)			
1	☐	☐	☐
2	☐	☐	☐
3	☐	☐	☐
Kitchen Furniture:			
Washing Machine	☐	☐	☐
Dishwasher	☐	☐	☐
Tumble-Drier	☐	☐	☐
Cooker	☐	☐	☐
Other (state which)			
1	☐	☐	☐

	INCLUDED IN THE SALE	EXCLUDED FROM THE SALE	NONE AT THE PROPERTY
2	☐	☐	☐
3	☐	☐	☐
Bathroom Fitments:			
Cabinet	☐	☐	☐
Towel Rails	☐	☐	☐
Soap and Tooth-brush Holders	☐	☐	☐
Toilet Roll Holders	☐	☐	☐
Fitted Shelves/ Cupboards	☐	☐	☐
Other Sanitary Fittings	☐	☐	☐
Shower			
Shower Fittings			
Shower Curtain			
Bedroom Fittings:			
Shelves	☐	☐	☐
Fitted Wardrobes	☐	☐	☐
Fitted Cupboards			
Fitted Shelving/ Cupboards			
Fitted Units			
Wall Mirrors			
Picture Hooks			
Plant Holders			
Clothes Line			
Rotary Line			

SPECIMEN

Please turn over to next page. PROP6/5

	INCLUDED IN THE SALE	EXCLUDED FROM THE SALE	NONE AT THE PROPERTY
Garden Shed			
Greenhouse			
Garden Ornaments			
Trees, Plants and Shrubs			
Garden Produce			
Stock of Oil/Solid Fuel/Propane Gas			
Water Butts			
Dustbins			
Other			

Signed Seller(s)

. . . .

. . . .

THE LAW SOCIETY

This form is part of The Law Society's TransAction scheme. © The Law Society 1992.
The Law Society is the professional body for solicitors in England and Wales.
January 1994

PROP6/6

GLOSSARY

ADVANCE
Money lent, usually by a building society or bank, to enable the borrower to purchase.

BRIDGING LOAN
A short term loan to complete the purchase of a property while the buyer is waiting for the sale of his home.

COLLATERAL
Property pledged as a guarantee for the repayment of money.

COMPLETION
The final legal transfer of ownership of the property.

CONTRACT
The written legal agreement between the seller and the purchaser with regard to the property.

CONVEYANCER
Solicitor or licensed conveyancer who arranges the legal aspects of buying and selling property.

CONVEYANCING
The legal work in the sale and purchase of property.

DEEDS
Legal documents entitling you to a property.

DISBURSEMENTS
The fees such as stamp duty, Land Registry fees and search fees which are payable to the conveyancer by the purchaser.

EASEMENT
A landowner's legal right to use the facilities of another's land, for example, a right of way.

EQUITY
The net value of mortgaged property after the mortgage has been deducted.

EXCHANGE OF CONTRACTS
The point when both purchaser and seller are legally bound to the transaction and the risk regarding the property passes to the purchaser.

FREEHOLD
Ownership of the property and the land on which it stands.

GROUND RENT
Annual charge payable by leaseholders to the freeholder.

HOME BUYERS' SURVEY AND VALUATION
Surveyor's report on a property – less extensive than a building survey.

INDEMNITY
Single payment for an insurance policy to cover the value of the property to lenders when they lend a high percentage of the purchase price.

JOINT TENANCY
Where two people – for example, husband and wife – hold half shares in a property. If one dies, the survivor takes all.

LAND REGISTRY FEES
Fees paid by the buyer to register evidence of ownership with the Land Registry. There is a scale of fees set by the government.

LEASE
Possession of property for the length of time fixed in the lease. This usually includes payment of an annual ground rent.

LEASEHOLD
Land held under a lease for a fixed number of years.

LESSEE
The person to whom a lease is granted.

LESSOR
The person who grants a lease.

MIRAS
Stands for Mortgage Interest Relief at Source. Now abolished.

MORTGAGE
A loan made against the secutiry of the property.

MORTGAGEE
The financial institution lending the money.

MORTGAGOR
The person borrowing the money.

QUALIFIED VALUER
A valuer who has passed advanced examinations and is bound by a strict code of professional conduct (look for the letters ARICS, FRICS).

REDEMPTION
The final payment on a mortgage. Some building societies make a charge (redemption fee) if a mortgage is ended earlier than was first agreed.

REINSTATEMENT VALUE
The cost of demolishing a house and rebuilding it including all associated legal and design fees.

STAMP DUTY
Government tax payable on the purchase of a property above a certain selling price.

SUBJECT TO CONTRACT
Wording of any agreement before the exchange of

contracts which allows either
party to withdraw without
incurring a penalty.

SURVEY
Inspection of the property by
an independent surveyor normally on behalf of the intending
purchaser.

TERM
The length of time over which
the mortgage loan is to be
repaid.

VALUATION
Inspection of the property to
ascertain its acceptability to the
lender as security against the
mortgage loan.

VENDOR
The person selling a property.

ADDRESSES FOR FURTHER INFORMATION

Society of Licensed Conveyancers, 55 Church Road, Croydon, CR9 1PF (0181 681 1001)

Law Society, 113 Chancery Lane, London WC2A 1PL (0171 242 1222)

The Nationwide, Nationwide House, Pipers Way, Swindon SN38 1XX (01793 456374)

The Halifax, Trinity Road, Halifax, West Yorks HX1 2RG (01422 333333)

Royal Institution of Chartered Surveyors, 12 Great George Street, Parliament Sq., London SW1P 3AD (0171 222 7000)

National Association of Estate Agents, Arbon House, 21 Jury Street, Warwick, CV34 4EH (01926 496800)

Building Societies Association/Council of Mortgage Lenders, 3 Savile Row, London W1X 1AF (0171 437 0655)

National House Building Council, Chiltern Avenue, Amersham, Bucks HP6 5AP (01494 434477)

Leasehold Enfranchisement Advisory Service, 6–8 Maddox Street, London W1R 9PN (0171 493 3116)

Ombudsman for Estate Agents, Beckett House, 4 Bridge St., Salisbury, Wiltshire SP1 2LX (01722 333306)

Building Societies Ombudsman, Millbank Tower, Millbank, London, SW1P 4XS (0171 931 0044)

YOUR PERSONAL ADDRESSES AND TELEPHONE NUMBERS

ESTATE AGENT

Telephone No.

SURVEYOR

Telephone No.

MORTGAGE COMPANY

Telephone No.

INSURANCE COMPANY: BUILDINGS

Telephone No.

INSURANCE COMPANY: CONTENTS

Telephone No.

REMOVAL COMPANY

Telephone No.

ELECTRIC COMPANY

Telephone No.

WATER COMPANY

Telephone No.
SOLICITOR

Telephone No.
MORTGAGE BROKER

Telephone No.
ENDOWMENT COMPANY

Telephone No.
GAS COMPANY

Telephone No.
COUNCIL OFFICES

Telephone No.
TELEPHONE COMPANY

Telephone No.

INDEX